Text © 2005 M-C McInally and Eric Summers

Design & layout © 2005 Leckie & Leckie

1st edition 2005, reprinted 2005, 2006

Mind Map is a registered trademark of the Buzan Organisation Ltd. Tony Buzan is the originator of Mind Maps®.

ISBN 1-84372-280-1

ISBN-13: 978-1-84372-280-9

Published by
Leckie & Leckie
3rd Floor
4 Queen Street
Edinburgh
EH2 1JF

T: 0131 220 6831

F: 0131 225 9987
E: enquiries@leckieandleckie.co.uk
W: www.leckieandleckie.co.uk

Special thanks to
Roda Morrison (proofreading), The Partnership Publishing Solutions Ltd (design and page make-up), Caleb Rutherford (cover design), Hamish Sanderson (illustrations), Teviotdale Publishing Solutions (project consultancy and editing).

Printed by Ashford Colour Press

A CIP Catalogue record for this book is available from the British Library.

CONTENTS

Introduction   5

Chapter 1   Brain Compatible Learning: the amazing brain   **7**

Learning styles   7
The amazing human brain   9
Multi-sensory learning   17
Emotional intelligence   27

Chapter 2   Mind, Body, Fitness and Environment   **33**

Exercise   33
Eating and drinking   39
Choosing your workspace   48
Increasing your confidence   50

Chapter 3   Study Techniques   **55**

Reading   55
Note-taking   59
Remembering   69
Doing past papers   70

Chapter 4   Time Management   **80**

How much time do I have?   80
Time management crutches   85
Getting it right...   92

Further reading   96

Introduction

What this book is about

This book is all about doing well in exams and fulfilling our potential.

Almost all of us would like to be better than we are. We wish we could be fitter and healthier, better company, more knowledgeable, and generally just more successful.

There are a lucky few who seem to have it all. This book is for the rest of us. We often have bad days, we are sometimes lonely, we worry about our health, we don't always get picked for sports' events and we fail exams. We think…we know…we could do better but we are not sure how to go about improving things.

So what this book does is draw upon what has been learned over the years about improving our health, our reading and our thinking skills, and, most importantly for exams, our memory. People who improve all these things feel good about themselves and raise their self-esteem.

The chapters which follow make use of scientific research but also common sense and the everyday experiences of teachers and students. It will acknowledge that hard work does not come easily to most of us, but it will provide tips and advice on how to overcome natural laziness and how to go about things more efficiently.

How this book is organised

Chapter 1 is about how the brain works. You will learn that different people have different learning preferences. There are exercises to help you understand how your brain works and this will help guide your study arrangements.

Study skills
and Strategies

371.30281

D0227039

M-C McInally   Eric Summers

Chapter 2 is about health. It explains how mental and physical fitness go together and suggests some very easy exercises that you can follow and meals, quick to prepare, which will sustain you through your weeks of exam preparation.

Chapter 3 is about the study basics of reading, note-taking and tackling exam questions.

Chapter 4 is about time management because being a teenager is not just about studying. It is also about leading a full life and making the most of every day.

Between the chapters are a few brief biographies of famous Scots. When we look at the lives of famous people, there are always lessons we can learn for our own lives. These Scots have shown just how much can be achieved with the right attitude.

Here now are questions to ask yourself. Do you want to do better? Do you wish to pass your exams? Are you willing to work hard?

If you are answering *Yes*, then swallow hard, take a deep breath and turn to Chapter 1.

BRAIN COMPATIBLE LEARNING
The amazing brain

In recent years a great deal has been found out about how the brain works and how it can be used to study more efficiently. In this chapter, you will read about:

- Learning styles and how to work out which is best for you.
- Gender differences and how they can affect learning.
- The structure of the brain and why it matters.
- Multi-sensory learning which can help you remember so much more.
- Multiple intelligences because people have a great range of talents and…
- Emotional intelligence because it can help us cope with difficulties (including exams) and lead happier lives.

LEARNING STYLES

Over 80% of what we know about the brain function has been learned in the last 15 years. With the help of advanced medical technology, neuro-scientists can now tell us how this amazing organ both learns and remembers. Using such new knowledge, this chapter will help you understand your own learning style, challenging and empowering you to achieve greater academic success.

What are learning styles?

Right from when you enter primary school, the way you learn will depend very much on your gender. Some neuro-scientists have produced quite persuasive reports from their research to say that boys approach work differently from girls. Now, do you feel better knowing that? Or did you already know it but didn't have the proof to tell your mum or dad when they compared you with a brother or a sister?

Given the choice, boys usually spend time with other boys and like noisy play and interaction which can be quite physical and competitive. Girls usually enjoy talking with friends, preferring quieter activities and working together in a cooperative way.

Don't worry if you are reading this and thinking it doesn't quite describe the way you are. Remember that we are all different and we don't always conform to generalised ideas. If you are a quiet cooperative young man or a noisy physical young woman just bear this in mind when you're investigating the right learning style for your personality. There are biological differences in the male and female brains and those differences affect the way we learn and behave. A simplistic overview of this is:

The male approach to learning

- males tend to be quite focussed
- males are generally good at solving 3-dimensional puzzles
- males are generally noisy, competitive, and aggressive
- males need early success in order to stay on-task
- males can tend to be greater risk takers.

The female approach to learning

- females place more emphasis on communication and collaboration
- females are more able to work alone or with one or two friends
- females are more able to undertake several tasks or instructions at the same time
- females are more able to listen to instructions
- females can tend to keep emotions and behaviour under control.

If you are interested in this area and want to learn more there is a huge amount of literature available on the subject. Two popular books are *Men are from Mars and Women are from Venus* and *Why Men Don't Iron*.

Your learning style is influenced by your gender, but it is also affected by other factors like the type of environment you are learning in and social groupings. It is important for you to identify what helps you learn better. To do this, you need to understand your own learning profile.

Brain-based research has produced notions of *whole brain learning, accelerated learning, multiple intelligences* and *emotional intelligence.* The combined message from this research is that the human brain loves learning; the more the brain learns, the more it is capable of learning. If you want to improve your ability to learn you must take into account the whole person. This includes your motives for learning, your personal values and your preferred learning style.

Remember:
Different people learn in different ways. Find out what suits you best.

THE AMAZING HUMAN BRAIN

We take information about the world in through our five senses, which give us the ability to hear, smell, touch, see and taste. It is important that we learn to appreciate which of our senses we rely on most for our learning and learn to use them efficiently (you will see how you use your senses in mind-mapping in Chapter 3). It is also equally important to train ourselves to use all our senses in our learning, so we can become better learners and gain greater experience.

On average, we only use between 1% – 4% of our brain's potential. This means we have a whole lot of potential we could be using. To see how best to unlock some of that, let's look at the structure of this amazing organ and give you a greater understanding to help you achieve your potential.

There are three layers to the brain – known as the triune brain.

The top layer (neocortex) – is the thinking part. It is split into two hemispheres, the right and the left.

The middle layer (limbic) – is the emotions part. It deals with our sense of identity and values, and with long term memory.

The lower layer (reptilian) – is the survival part, controlling all body functions and instincts.

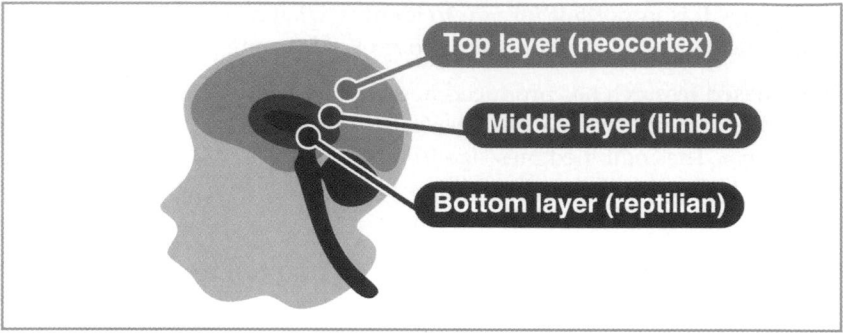

Human brain showing: a) top layer (neocortex); b) middle brain (limbic); c) bottom layer (reptilian).

To learn effectively it is important to work the layers of the brain to get the best out of them. This book will help you to do this.

The top layer

The top layer comprises 80% of the whole brain. It is involved in:

- thinking and problem solving
- speaking and language development
- reasoning and creative thought
- behaviour.

The top layer of the brain consists of two halves, the left and right hemispheres. The left and right hemispheres have different characteristics, with the left hemisphere being associated with logical

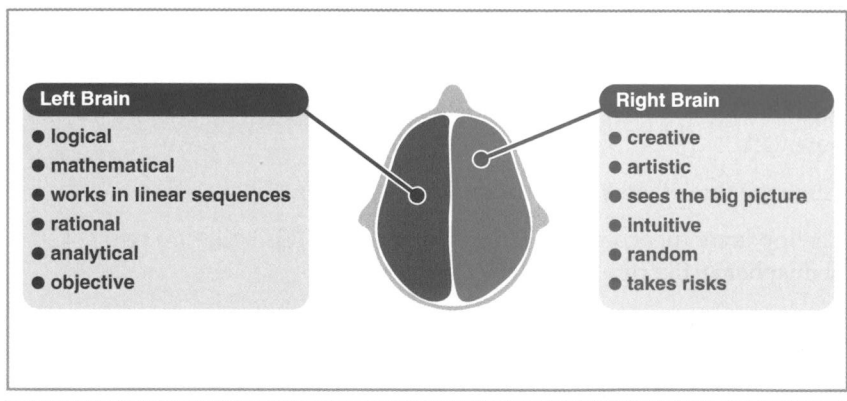

Left Brain
- logical
- mathematical
- works in linear sequences
- rational
- analytical
- objective

Right Brain
- creative
- artistic
- sees the big picture
- intuitive
- random
- takes risks

Left-hand and right-hand brain, with preferences.

processes, and the right hemisphere being associated with creative processes. We all use both sides of the brain to a greater or lesser degree, but most people have a natural preference for one hemisphere over the other. In other words, we are likely to respond in either a *logical* or *creative* way to different learning experiences. Really effective thinking and learning uses both sides of the brain. If you know which side you prefer, you can learn to use your brain more effectively.

Left-brain learners prefer	Right-brain learners prefer
■ Structure	■ Open-ended tasks
■ Being organised	■ Looking at the 'big picture', the whole task
■ Explicit instructions	
■ Written information	■ Self-selected tasks
■ Working in a linear way, e.g. first point then second point, etc.	■ Working from intuition, guesses, hunches
■ Checking their work	■ Hands-on experience
■ Reading and writing	■ Learning by demonstration/role play/seeing a video
■ Following instructions	
■ Working to deadlines	■ Making own deadlines as they may find imposed ones difficult to meet
■ Being logical	
	Right-brain learners may appear disorganised

Are you a left or right hemisphere learner?

Most people use both sides of the brain to a greater or larger extent. But, most of us have a preference for one hemisphere. Are you mostly right or mostly left?

Answer the questionnaire to see your hemisphere preference on the next two pages to find out.

Read the following pairs of statements and quickly decide whether statement a) or statement b) is the better description of you. Mark your response by circling the appropriate letter.

1   If you were doing a jigsaw puzzle, would be more likely to:
    a) sort all the pieces into categories (corners, straight bits, sky, etc.)?
    b) begin by sorting the edges and corners but fit bits together as you spot them?

2   Which box would you more readily pair with Box 1:
    a) Box 2?
    b) Box 3?

| *pig* | *car* | *cow* |

3   When you buy a new appliance (camera, phone, MP3 player, etc), would you be more likely to:
    a) briefly examine the instruction booklet and experiment?
    b) carefully read and follow the instructions?

4   If you were going on holiday, would you prefer to:
    a) plan what you are doing well in advance?
    b) book at the last minute and perhaps get a bargain?

5   Do you have hunches about the future or how things will turn out:
    a) fairly often?
    b) hardly ever?

6   When you are writing a letter or typing an essay, do you:
    a) regularly check your work and carefully read what you have written?
    b) find checking your work a bit of a chore?

7   Is your work area:
    a) usually organised and you can find things easily?
    b) untidy so you have to search through a muddle to find anything?

8 When you are given a task with a deadline, do you:
   a) usually plan in advance and beat the deadline?
   b) only really get stuck in as the deadline gets close?

9 Which box would you more readily match with Box 1?
   a) Box 2?
   b) Box 3?

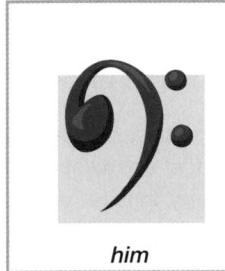
him

her

ten

10 When faced with a problem, would you say you tend to:
   a) get a feel for the situation and possible solutions?
   b) gather and analyse the facts so that you understand the situation better?

11 When you are tackling a project are you more likely to:
   a) make a few notes to start with?
   b) establish an outline and structure the main issues, themes and tasks?

12 Do you prefer to:
   a) read the book and then decide whether you will see the film?
   b) see the film?

Give yourself 1 point each time you:
answered a) to questions 2, 3, 5, 10 and 11;
answered b) to questions 1, 4, 6, 7, 8, 9, 12.

Now mark your score on the scale:

| L | | 1 | 2 | 3 | 4 | 5 | 6 | 7 | 8 | 9 | 10 | 11 | 12 | | R |

Your score shows whether you are mostly left- or right-brained in your learning style. If you score from 1 to 4, you are a left-brain learner. If you score from 9 to 12, you are a right-brain learner, and if you score in the middle, you are a balanced left- and right-brain learner.

Knowing whether you are a left-brain learner or a right-brain learner helps you create a good learning profile for yourself. You can now use this new knowledge to understand he best way for you to tackle your studying.

Do you need that structured study plan that the teachers and your parents love? If you are left-brained the answer is yes.

But, the answer is also yes if you are right-brained because you need the bigger picture and like to self-select your own tasks. The truth is you just tackle the task differently!

Left-brain people will follow the logical steps and approach the study plan with the subject they think they need to revise most or the subject that has the most content will be spread over the whole revision period.

Right-brained people will study what they enjoy most and give time for mind-maps and concept maps or studying Leckie & Leckie Success Guides on the computer rather than from the textbook.

If you're mostly left-brained:

you need:	*because:*
structure	you like order and cannot work efficiently in chaos
explicit instructions	you like direction
written information	you like to re-read information to clarify and check your work
working in linear manner	you like to go through tasks step by step.

You are the type of person who reads the instruction manual before assembling the item or using the equipment. You are also more likely to be patient and plan tasks in detail, and you are what is called a finisher as you will start a task and see it through to the end.

- Left-brained people tend to analyse everything and think or work out every possible consequence before embarking on a task.
- Left-brained people do not like to learn in an environment that does not have good order.
- Left-brain people will have good notes, in order, and possibly rewritten with colour coding to aid learning.

If you're mostly right-brained:

you need:	*because:*
open-ended tasks	you make previous connections to prior learning
the big picture	it allows you to get an overview of the whole process
self-selecting tasks	it allows you the chance to learn with others in groupwork or on your own
to work from intuition	it allows you the chance to learn by discovery.

You are the type of person who will only look briefly at the instruction manual when you get a new piece of equipment, and even then, you'll only look at the manual when you can't get something to work.

- Right-brained people tend to live for the moment and not think too much about the consequences.
- Right-brained people like to use their creativity and imagination when tackling tasks.
- Right-brained people are often regarded for their ideas, they are good at brainstorming exercises but are not always good at following through to the end of the task.
- Right-brained people feel uncomfortable with tight deadlines and may experience stress.
- Right-brained people should incorporate videos, graphs, mind-maps, computers, colour and music into their studying.

It is important to acknowledge that the more we try to use both sides of our brain the more effective we will be at learning. It is easy to say 'I can't do that!' but if you do that too often you are already processing the brain to failure.

It is best to try and see the big picture but also realise that the task has to be broken down into manageable tasks that have a time limit for completion.

Tips to keep the top layer/neocortex brain happy:

1 make the connections from one lesson/lecture to the other

2 provide input to all the senses

3 concentrate in short bursts

4 use role play/guided visualisation/music to help you work better

5 use a variety of learning materials, e.g. video, notes, ICT

6 ask for regular feedback from peers or a teacher.

The middle layer

The middle layer of the brain responds to our five senses, deciding if the information it receives is of value or not. The middle layer determines our emotions. It is the area where our values and beliefs and our sense of identity is rooted. Our long-term memory is held here and associated with our emotions. The more powerful a memory is linked to an emotion the greater the possibility of recalling it for future use. This area is rich in *neurotransmitters* which help to transport the messages throughout the brain. This area includes the endorphins – natural opiates which kill pain and make us feel good. It is vital that you are motivated to learn as this positively engages the emotions and maximises the ability to pay attention, to understand meaning and allow for the all important recall.

Tips to keep the middle layer/limbic brain happy:

1 *What's in it for me?* Ask yourself that question every time you learn something new.

2 *Connect in to your values* What will be exciting enough for you to pay attention, that you consider interesting and important?

3 *Recognition of achievement* The limbic brain loves to be told it's doing a good job.

4 *Getting feedback* The limbic brain also loves to be told how it can do an even better job.

The bottom layer

The bottom layer of the brain is located at the brain stem and is the most primitive part of the brain. It is also known as the reptilian brain. It controls all the basic body functions such as breathing, heart beat, blood pressure, balance and body temperature. It is responsible for your survival responses of *flight* or *fright* in the face of danger.

Under physical threat, stress or anxiety the brain stops learning and downshifts into survival mode. For example, if you find yourself in the face of an angry charging tiger, do you run away, or do you stay and fight it? The answer to that one may be obvious, but there are other cases where you might think you have a chance of winning if you stay and fight. This is where your middle layer needs to connect with the bottom layer and bring in your value systems to make a judgement for you.

The bottom layer holds certain instinctive behaviours like the pecking order, rote behaviour and conformity to social trends in your culture. The most important task for this layer is survival in any threatening situation. If the brain finds itself under threat, whether physical, emotional or psychological, the reptilian brain will take control. So for learning to take place the reptilian brain has to be happy that all is well.

Tips to keep the bottom layer/reptilian brain happy:

1 have your own territorial learning space – a locker/drawer/shelf
2 be comfortable when you are learning – not hungry/too hot/too cold
3 have rules to follow for your learning – set patterns, e.g. allocated tasks
4 feel safe when you are learning both physically and emotionally
5 keep your self-esteem high (*see* Chapter 2)
6 reduce stress levels (*see* Chapter 2).

MULTI-SENSORY LEARNING

It is generally recognised that in multi-sensory learning there are three main systems of learning:

Visual or Verbal learning is driven by images.
The visual learner says 'I see what you mean' or 'That looks like a good idea'.

Auditory learning is driven by sounds.
The auditory learner says 'That rings a bell' or 'That sounds like a good idea'.

Kinaesthetic learning is driven by movement and feelings.
The kinaesthetic learner says 'I've got the hang of this' or 'That feels right to me'.

Collectively, these are called VAK systems. Different types of learners will respond best to different types of stimuli or sources of information.

Visually/Verbally-oriented learners respond well to:

- written word
- diagrams/pictures
- films/TV/videos
- wall charts.

Auditorily-oriented learners respond well to:

- spoken word
- lectures
- discussions
- audio tapes.

Kinaesthetically-oriented learners respond well to:

- movement/acting
- hands on activities
- design/drawing
- writing
- practising the skill while receiving instruction.

Of course, we all use all three systems of learning, but we usually rely more on one than the other two. If you understand VAK systems, you can make them work for you.

Each person has a learning style as unique as their fingerprint. Our learning style is characterised by the way we interact with the environment, taking in, filtering and processing data in order to learn. Our learning style is made up of our hemisphere preference, our VAK style, our physical and psychological preferences and intelligence profile. All this makes up our learning profile.

Remember:
The brain is very complex, but an understanding of how it works can give you more control over your learning and your behaviour.

Multiple intelligences

There are lots of ways in which intelligence can be measured. Usually, people think that their IQ measures their intelligence, but there are many aspects to intelligence which are not always properly measured using standard IQ tests.

There is now a theory of multiple intelligences, developed by Dr Howard Gardner of Harvard University in the USA. In this theory, there are at least seven different types of intelligence, none of which is fixed and all capable of being developed and expanded. Each type of intelligence has a number of characteristics, and by identifying which characteristics correspond to elements of the way your brain works, you can work out your strengths and weaknesses when it comes to learning. Knowing your weaknesses also means you can identify activities which will help improve these types of intelligence.

Have a look at the table on the next page and see if you can pick out your own types of intelligence.

Intelligence type	Characteristics
Linguistic *Vocabulary clever*	Enjoys words (reading, writing, speaking) Will speak publicly Selects appropriate vocabulary Can use words to present a point of view persuasively Expresses themselves clearly using words
Mathematical/logical *Number clever*	Can recognise patterns and understand them Enjoys puzzles Is comfortable using formulae to solve problems Enjoys science Likes logical structured approaches to problems
Visual/spatial *Image clever*	Likes to draw and doodle Enjoys constructing models Can follow instructions more easily Can 'see' in their mind a problem and its solution
Musical *Musically clever*	Enjoys listening to music Is often found singing or whistling May tap feet or fingers Can follow a rhythm
Bodily/kinaesthetic *Body Movement clever*	Likes to move around Has good coordination Uses gestures and movement to express themselves Skilled sportsperson
Interpersonal *People clever*	Can communicate easily with people Works well in a group or team Reads people well High in Emotional Intelligence
Intrapersonal *Self clever*	Is comfortable to explore their own feelings and emotions Can identify their own strengths and weaknesses

Can you identify with your intelligence types? Try this profile questionnaire to find out what style of learner you are and help start the journey to successful learning.

Multiple intelligence profile

Read each statement carefully and assess on a scale of 1 to 5 how well each statement describes you. Score 5 if you strongly agree with the statement, and 1 if you strongly disagree. Write your score for each statement and add the scores for each section.

Strongly agree	Agree	Neither agree nor disagree	Disagree	Strongly disagree
5	4	3	2	1

Section A
I find it easy to express myself in writing ....

I find it easy to follow a lecture or written article ....

I have a large vocabulary ....

I am good at explaining things to others ....

Total ....

Section B
I have a feeling for working with numbers ....

I am good at picking out patterns ....

I enjoy problem solving ....

I like to work through a task in a logical, orderly manner ....

Total ....

Section C
I am good at map reading ....

I find it easy to do puzzles which involve rotating shapes ....

I can hold an image in my mind ....

I find graphs/diagrams helpful in understanding information ....

Total ....

Section D
I can remember a tune easily ....

I can play a musical instrument ....

I can easily pick out different instruments playing in an orchestral piece

I enjoy spending time listening to or making music ....

Total ....

Section E
I like working with my hands ....

I find it difficult to sit still for long ....

I enjoy physical activity and have good coordination ....
I prefer hands-on learning to reading or listening ....
Total ....

Section F
I work well in a team ....
I have a lot of empathy with others ....
I enjoy mixing with other people ....
I am good at talking people into doing things ....
Total ....

Section G
I am self-motivated ....
I an good at controlling my moods ....
I am aware of my own behaviour ....
Total ....

Your relative intelligence assessment:

Section A	Section B	Section C	Section D	Section E	Section F	Section G
20	20	20	20	20	20	20
19	19	19	19	19	19	19
18	18	18	18	18	18	18
17	17	17	17	17	17	17
16	16	16	16	16	16	16
15	15	15	15	15	15	15
14	14	14	14	14	14	14
13	13	13	13	13	13	13
12	12	12	12	12	12	12
11	11	11	11	11	11	11
10	10	10	10	10	10	10
9	9	9	9	9	9	9
8	8	8	8	8	8	8
7	7	7	7	7	7	7
6	6	6	6	6	6	6
5	5	5	5	5	5	5
4	4	4	4	4	4	4
3	3	3	3	3	3	3
2	2	2	2	2	2	2
1	1	1	1	1	1	1
Linguistic	*Mathematical/ logical*	*Visual/ spatial*	*Musical*	*Bodily/ kinaesthetic*	*INTER- personal*	*INTRA- personal*

Check your answers next to the sections and see for yourself where you fit in and try to work out areas you need to work on to improve your score. For example, if you scored highly (between 15 and 20) in Section A, you are strong in Linguistic intelligence, but if you scored low (between 1 and 5) in Section C, you are weak in Visual and spatial intelligence.

Knowing your strengths can help you adapt the way you do things to make the most of these strengths. At the same time, it helps to know what your weaknesses are to make sure you don't rely too much on them in difficult or important situations.

It is important to realise that you can improve your score in any of the intelligences, if you are willing to practise. Many jobs will rely on the characteristics found in the different intelligences, so it is important to recognise this and try to improve, especially if the characteristic is in your chosen field of study.

The list below shows the relationships between different characteristics and different jobs, and suggest some activities which can help you strengthen those characteristics.

Linguistic
Found in writers, journalists, teachers and TV presenters

Try these activities to strengthen your linguistic intelligence:

- brainstorming, debates, discussion, speaking to an audience
- writing letters, stories, diaries, poetry, lists, reading, extracting information from text
- word games and puzzles
- telling jokes and riddles.

Mathematical and Logical
Found in scientists, engineers, accountants, doctors, mathematicians

Try these activities to strengthen your mathematical and logical intelligence:

- try to use mental arithmetic and not reach for the calculator
- be aware of numbers in your environment, e.g. bus numbers, car registrations, speed restrictions, timetables for trains, buses and aeroplanes
- ask you teacher to go over problem-solving techniques
- learn to recognise patterns
- practise code making/breaking.

Visual and Spatial
Found in artists, engineers, architects, footballers, landscape gardeners
Try these activities to strengthen your visual and spatial intelligence:

- reading maps
- drawing graphs
- mind-mapping/concept mapping
- using your imagination
- guided visualisation
- artwork, sculpture, model making.

Musical
Found in musicians, sound technicians, recording technicians
Try these activities to strengthen your musical intelligence:

- play musical instruments
- make music
- singing, rapping
- rhythm activities, e.g. drumming
- use music when studying to enhance your mood.

Bodily and Kinaesthetic
Found in athletes, actors, dancers, surgeons, designers
Try these activities to strengthen your bodily and kinaesthetic intelligence:

- drama
- dance
- sport
- field trips
- role play games.

Interpersonal
Found in teachers, managers, counsellors, human resources, politicians
Try these activities to strengthen your interpersonal intelligence:

- team work and group work
- peer tutoring
- team games
- giving and receiving feedback and constructive criticism
- group discussions and projects.

Intrapersonal

Found in philosophers, novelists, psychiatrists, psychologists, forensic scientists

Try these activities to strengthen your intrapersonal intelligence:

■ personal target setting
■ keeping a diary/journal
■ learn study skills
■ self-evaluation.

Your own learning profile

By now you should be getting a pretty clear picture of what is your personal learning profile:

■ you have your left-/right-brain hemisphere
■ you have your VAK system
■ you have your intelligence type.

Make use of your learning style when you revise:

Visual Learner	Auditory Learner	Kinaesthetic Learner
Rewrite your notes as Mind-maps	Read your notes to yourself	Copy out your notes. Write down from memory key points
Use colour to highlight points	Read your notes silently Learn to 'self-talk'	Move around the room when you are revising
Draw diagrams and sketches to help you remember points	Record yourself reading key points – use later when out for a jog/walk	Revise while you do exercise – literally 'jog' your memory
Rewrite your key points using different words	Revise with friends or a 'study buddy'	Mentally review what you have been revising
Use computer revision programs	Make up notes to a favourite tune	Place key points about your room/home

It is now up to you to use the identified strengths, in each of the intelligences. If you remember to practise them you'll help yourself get better grades. Most people will have areas that they are good in, and other areas they are less good in. What is important is knowing your own strengths and weaknesses and having control over how to improve.

Remember: Intelligence can express itself in a range of ways. Know what you are good at; work at what you would like to do better.

EMOTIONAL INTELLIGENCE

Daniel Goleman is a famous American scientist who has done a lot of research on emotional intelligence, which he describes as *'a different way of being smart'*. It compliments in many ways Gardner's interpersonal and intrapersonal intelligences. Remember the middle layer of the brain (the limbic) works better when emotion is tied into the learning process.

It is a bit like if we combine all the elements in our *intrapersonal skills* and *interpersonal skills,* to make us more aware of ourselves and others around us. Goleman believes we cannot achieve our full potential as learners until we have mastered emotional intelligence. He argues that to be emotionally intelligent we need to be self-aware, meaning that you need to be able to identify and acknowledge your own feelings and use them when you are making decisions. If you are emotionally intelligent it is more likely that you are a better self-manager, motivated, resilient, optimistic and more in control of your moods. This can be difficult, especially if you have scored low in either interpersonal or intrapersonal skills. So, can we overcome this? As we said at the beginning it might take some hard work.

Aristotle said: *'Any one can become angry – that is easy. But to be angry with the right person, to the right degree, at the right time, for the right purpose, and in the right way – this is not easy.'*

We can all recount a time when we got it wrong with someone. What is not always easy is firstly to admit that we *got it wrong*, and secondly to make sure we don't get it wrong again. We all could do better in this world if we improved our emotional intelligence.

To improve your understanding of emotional intelligence, you must first know what you are looking for. How to recognise if you are emotionally intelligent?

Do you:

- care what other people are feeling or going through?
- control your impulses and manage emotions, i.e. can you handle anger? or jealousy?
- display compassion to others?
- recognise feelings and name them?
- respect differences in how people think about things?
- evaluate your own strengths and weaknesses and address any issues?
- listen to other people before barging into conversation?
- cooperate with others or is it your way or no way?
- take responsibility for your actions and take control of your life?
- think positively?

If the answer to some of the above was 'no' or 'don't know' then you need to think a bit more about the way you deal with your emotions, both with yourself and with other people.

Values and attitudes and why they are important to your learning

Your values are the beliefs you have about the way you think people should behave and the principles which govern the way you live your life – what you think is right and wrong, good and bad, desirable and undesirable.

Everyone has values but not all people share the same values. It is therefore up to you to decide what values you want to hold on to or to adopt as you mature and experience more of life. Some of your values will come from your parents or teachers or from your culture. Once you acknowledge where your values come from, you are in a position to reflect on them and work out the important beliefs and values you hold.

These values and beliefs will have an effect on how you approach your study.

Do you value hard work, the truth, being kind to others, not being selfish, not breaking the law, looking after yourself, being the best you can be? Think about these values and consider how many you share with your friends and family. Think about the way you relate to other people and the ways other people relate to you and how these relationships are affected by your values and their values.

Take time to care about people and other things in your life apart from yourself and wait and see the effects of your efforts. It is true that you get a feel-good factor when you help a friend or a stranger. It is important to feel good about yourself and helping others and caring for others will help you do this. It seems commonsense, but it's not always the easiest thing to do, and sometimes this means that adolescents get branded as being selfish. It is also important for you to start getting your values set out and living by them, even if it is not always an easy thing to do. Ask most adults what their values are and they will have to think hard and rediscover what is important to them.

Emotional intelligence is about :

self-awareness
- recognising how your feelings affect you
- knowing your limitations and strengths
- knowing where you need to improve and asking for help
- monitoring 'self-talk', keeping yourself right

self-management
- finding ways to manage and control your emotions through suitable outlets (e.g. playing sport, watching TV, listening to music)
- taking responsibility for decisions and actions
- being flexible, giving you the ability to adapt to new challenges
- being motivated, knowing your goals and working towards them
- learning the difference between assertiveness and aggression

social awareness
- being a good listener
- empathising with others
- recognising others' feelings and allowing them their perspective

relationship
management

- being a good team worker – learning when to lead and when to follow
- inspiring others
- preventing conflict in the group or with others
- being interested in other people

Trying to master your emotional intelligence will not only make you better to be with but will also help you to become a better person. When you are at this stage in your education you are constantly learning new concepts and information. Try to keep an open mind to new ideas, other peoples' experiences and how they could improve your experiences. Remember employers may look for the qualifications first as an indication of intelligence, but when it comes to promotion, emphasis is placed on interpersonal skills and problem-solving skills.

How will emotional intelligence help with studying and learning, and passing exams? Being emotionally intelligent will help you be:

- more confident
- more effective with people and dealing with them
- better at sharing with others
- better at coping and developing strategies
- more motivated.

Remember:
Research suggests that people who are successful and happy in life tend to have high emotional intelligence. If you suspect you haven't got it, go and get it. It matters!

CHAPTER SUMMARY

What's In It For Me!

Some parts of this chapter may seem rather theoretical, but it really is worth your while getting to know how your brain functions because doing so will help you:

■ understand the learning styles which suit you best and enable you to study more efficiently

■ recognise the different types of intelligence, including your own

■ appreciate the crucial importance, especially at a time when you are coping with exam stress, of managing your emotions.

Think about it! If you can speed up your computer, you do. The brain is an astonishing natural computer and after reading this chapter you know how to make it run better. How foolish not to do so.

Kenny Dalglish was one of the greatest ever Scottish footballers. He was capped 102 times for his country and, along with Denis Law, holds the record for number of goals scored. He is a legendary Celtic player and at his second club, Liverpool, he is remembered as possibly the finest player ever to turn out for their team.

What made him so good? He was very strong, very skilful and he loved winning. He was a footballing genius. But there was much more to his success than simple talent. Another great player, Lou Macari, who starred alongside Dalglish at Celtic and for Scotland, recently said, 'There is no doubt that Kenny was a genius, but no one worked harder at his genius!'

This is true of so many great players. Alex Ferguson used to look out from his office at Old Trafford over the darkened pitch. One young boy would still be practising long after everyone else had left. That was David Beckham, already good but determined to become even better.

Gordon Strachan was a tremendously energetic, highly talented player who displayed remarkable levels of fitness long after others had retired. This author saw him play when he was in his mid 40s and he was still the best player on the park. The point is that Strachan looked after himself. Football was his trade, he knew he had to care for his body and he therefore always ensured that was in bed by 10.00pm when he was playing and he never touched alcohol.

It was the same with Dalglish. He was teetotal, never abused his body and was a great student of the game. As a result he was rarely injured and retained an enthusiasm and fitness level that astounded younger players.

The lesson: Great people work hard to be great. The rest of us could all achieve much more if we too understood that success comes with hard work. 10% inspiration, 90% perspiration.

MIND, BODY, FITNESS AND ENVIRONMENT

Your brain and your body are not separate. They are both you, and you will function better if you look after both. In this chapter you will learn:

- Simple exercises that will keep you in good physical shape.
- Healthy food (that even teenagers can prepare) which will ensure that mind and body are both well nourished.
- Where to study in an environment that is right for you.
- How to feel good about yourself so that you have the necessary confidence to tackle exams and cope with the stress that they sometimes bring.
- Where to go for help because all of us, at one time or another, need a hand.

EXERCISE

In order for your brain to work at its best, it's important for the rest of your body to be working properly – remember the reptilian brain? Try to make time every week for some exercise. It doesn't need to be anything too vigorous – walking to school instead of getting the bus, going for a swim or having a game of football with friends will help.

Getting the body working properly doesn't need to involve lots of time in the gym or out on the playing fields. There are plenty of easy exercises you can do in your bedroom or in the library, which help get your muscles and joints working and get the blood circulating a bit better round your body. Here are some simple exercises you can do which only take about 20 minutes. If you do these exercise three or four times a week, you'll start to notice a difference in the way your body feels after a few weeks.

Before you start the exercises, it's a good idea to do a bit of a warm-up. You can do this with five minutes of brisk walking or even climbing up and down the stairs. To do the exercises (right-brained people: you will need to look at the pictures and try to copy the pose)

- you'll need a chair, something to step onto (like a stair), and
- a pair of weights. (The weights don't need to be anything special – a bag of rice or a couple of cans of baked beans would do.)

Seated squat

1 Stand with your back to the front of a chair with your feet about hip-width apart

2 bend your knees slightly

3 extend your arms out in front of you, looking directly ahead

4 breathe in and bend your knees until your bottom touches the front of the chair – your knees should be bent at about 90°

5 keep your heels on the floor

6 breathe out and return to the starting position.

Repeat this 20 times.

Reverse flye

You need some weights for this one (or a can of soup/beans).

1 Stand with your feet hip-width apart and knees bent, but keep your back straight

2 lean forwards from the hips until you are looking down at the floor

3 hold the weights and let your arms hang down in front of you

4   breathe out and raise your arms up and out to the side – try to get your arms level with your shoulders, keeping your back straight and your knees bent

5   squeeze your shoulders together

6   breathe in and slowly lower your arms to the start position.

Repeat this 15 times.

Step-up
(go out for a break and find some stairs)

You need a step of about 15 cm for this one.

1   Stand facing the step, with your back straight

2   step up onto the step with your right foot

3   step up with your left foot – both feet should be flat on the step

4   step down, right foot first, then left foot.

Do this for a minute, then change over the leading foot for another minute.
Try to do the steps as quickly as you can without running out of breath.

Box press-up
(maybe better done in private this one)

1   Kneel on all fours, with your hands on the floor, just a bit wider than shoulder-width apart

2   keep your knees together on the floor and raise your feet in the air, crossing them at the ankles

3   breathe in and lower your body until your arms are bent at about 90°, keeping your back and your neck straight

4   breathe out and return to the starting position.

Repeat this one 20 times.

Power lunge

(easily done in between the bookshelves in the library!)

1 Stand upright with your feet hip-width apart

2 cross your hands across your chest so your hands are just below your shoulders

3 look straight ahead, and take a stride forwards with one foot – go forward about 60–90cm

4 breathe in and lower your back knee down towards the floor, and move your front knee forwards so it's directly above your front foot

5 breathe out and return to the starting position.

Do this for 30 seconds with one leg going forwards, then swap to the other leg.

Once you've done the full sequence of five exercises, repeat the cycle another two times. If you find these exercises getting easier, try increasing the number of times you do them on each cycle.

Desk exercises for the shy and retiring types

When you're studying, you'll be spending a lot of time sitting at your desk. However, if you spend too much time sitting, your muscles will start aching, and you won't be able to concentrate properly on what you're studying. Make a point of getting up every hour or so and moving around a bit. Make a cup of tea or do a few simple stretching exercises. It's a good idea to give the eyes a bit of a break too – sit with your eyes shut for a minute or two, or look out of the window to relieve them every so often.

Here are some simple exercises you can do while you're sitting at your desk which will help relieve stress and tension. You don't have to do all of them, but just pick a few at a time to help relax your muscles.

The neck

Sitting straight in your chair, slowly turn your head from side to side a few times, then hold it on the left for five seconds, and then move it right and hold it there for five seconds. Repeat this about five times. It's important that you do this exercise slowly, avoiding any sudden movement.

Shoulders

Lean forwards in your chair so your shoulders are away from the backrest. Hunch your shoulders – lift and rotate them backwards five times and then forwards five times. Try to increase the size of the movement each time, and repeat each direction about five times.

Upper back

Still leaning forwards slightly, let your arms hang down by your side. Keeping your elbows pointing down, swing your hands up so they are level with your shoulders. Push your shoulders back, stretching your upper chest and taking the strain off tight neck and shoulder muscles. Hold the shoulders back for ten seconds, and repeat this exercise five times.

Lower back

Move your chair away from the desk or turn it so that you have room to bend forwards. Sit upright with your feet and knees about a shoulder-width apart. Try to relax your body as much as you can, and slowly bend forward so your shoulders rest on your knees. You should do this very slowly, particularly if you've sitting in the same position for a long time and your muscles are particularly tight. Let your arms swing down and try to touch the floor with your fingers. Hold the position for five seconds and slowly straighten up in your chair. Repeat this exercise five times.

Fingers and wrists

If you spending a lot of time in front of the computer using a keyboard and mouse, your fingers and wrists will need a bit of a rest occasionally. The exercises above are necessary because you're sitting still and joints are getting stiff through a lack of movement. By contrast, your fingers need a rest because they're doing all the work and are probably being held in a single position as you type.

To exercise your fingers, sit straight in your chair, with your hands on your knees. Lift your hands from the knees, make a fist and then spread the fingers as wide as possible. Hold this position for five seconds and repeat the exercise five times.

To exercise the wrists, push the fingers of your right hand back towards the wrist using the palm of you left hand gently. Hold this position for five seconds. Repeat for the other hand and repeat the cycle five times.

Remember: Exercises do not have to be complicated or time-consuming, but they are important. Do them!

EATING AND DRINKING

To get the best out the brain and body, you need to make sure they get the right kind of fuel – food and water. Choosing the right foods can make a surprising difference to the way your brain works. You can also help yourself by making sure that you get the right fuel at the right times of the day, so that your body isn't crying out for food just when you need your brain to concentrate on studying.

Eating for an amazing brain

An essential part of making sure your body is working properly is eating properly. We all need to eat a balance of different foods. But often this is time consuming, and it is all too easy to become lazy and go for the 'junk food' fix. During adolescence is the time when your body does the most growing, and it needs the right combinations of calories, proteins, vitamins and minerals to make sure it grows properly and functions efficiently. Eating properly at this age also means you are likely to be healthier as you grow older.

A balanced diet
Different types of food can be classified into five basic food groups:

- bread, other cereals and potatoes
- fruit and vegetables
- milk and dairy foods
- meat, fish and alternatives
- foods containing fat and salt, foods and drinks containing sugar.

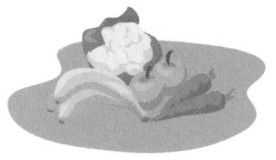  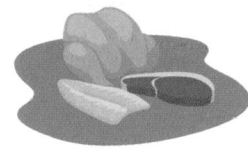

Healthy eating does not mean stopping eating what you have always eaten and changing to new expensive foods. It just means enjoying as wide a variety of foods as possible and getting a good balance.

To try to get the right balance of foods, choose foods from each of the five food groups in sensible proportions. All other foods and drinks are 'extras' which are not essential and should be kept to a minimum.

Filler foods

Filler foods should make up the main part of your meals. They include; bread (all kinds), potatoes, rice, pasta, breakfast cereals. Wholegrain varieties contain more fibre and are more filling.

Fruit and vegetables

Fruit and vegetables should be eaten at every meal and a good variety will give you most of the vitamins and minerals you need. Use any kind of fruit and vegetables, including fresh, frozen, tinned, dried and natural fruit juice.

Protein

Include a little protein at every meal. Foods which contain protein include fish, meat, eggs, milk, yoghurt, cheese, nuts and seeds, beans, lentils, and peanut butter. Your portions of these foods will be smaller than the filler foods, and you should try to eat a variety for a good balance. Some sources of protein, such as fish, nuts and seeds are high in Omega–6 fats, which are essential for brain development.

One particularly important mineral in your diet should be iron. It's been shown in a number of research studies that iron deficiencies have an adverse effect on academic performance. Up to 13% of teenage boys and girls were found to be low in iron; this may be due to rapid growth, poor diets and lifestyle choices. Good sources of iron are meat, green vegetables, and dried fruit like dates, figs and raisins. If you don't eat meat, try to add other things into your diet that are high in iron.

Caffeine (in tea, coffee and some soft drinks) lowers the amount of iron that can be absorbed. A lack of Vitamin C (found in oranges, blackcurrants, green leafy vegetables) also lowers the amount of iron that can be absorbed. Take a glass of orange juice with your meal to aid absorption.

Breakfast

It's really important to start the day with a decent breakfast. Skipping breakfast means your energy levels will be low throughout the day, and your ability to concentrate and learn will be affected. Always try to make time for breakfast. Use breakfast cereal bars to get you started if you normally do not eat breakfast.

Snacks

When you're in a rush, it's easy to skip meals. Skipping meals a few times isn't going to cause great problems as long as it does not become a habit, but it's important not to do it too regularly. Remember, food is the fuel your body needs to keep it going, so without enough of the right kind of food, you'll get run down and run out of energy too quickly.

If you're spending a lot of time in the library or your bedroom studying, it's a good idea to have a few snacks to keep you going, but it's important to have the right kind of snacks. Crisps and chocolates might be tempting, and they're alright in moderation, but they're not the best things to keep your brain working at its top performance. If you need  something to nibble on while you're studying, try some nuts and raisins, or some dried fruit – they have good combinations of vitamins and minerals, without having too much sugar.

For something a bit more substantial than nuts and raisins, here are some ideas for some easy snacks you can make quickly. You will often find you are studying when everyone else in the family is out, at work, or enjoying themselves, so you need to take responsibility for yourself. (Remember to try to combine foods from filler foods, fruit and vegetables and protein).

Bread, rolls, pitta bread, chapati with fillings of:
- fish – tuna, sardines, pilchards
- eggs – egg salad or hard boiled eggs
- lean cold meats – slices, wedges or cubes
- cheese – all kinds, especially low-fat
- peanut butter
- banana
- vegetables – tomato, lettuce, peppers, humous, cucumber.

Soups:
- add milk to tinned soups
- try split pea or lentil soup
- eat with bread, crispbread or crackers.

Baked potato with fillings:
- tuna mixed with green pepper, tomato and onion
- chopped bacon and pineapple
- tomato and sardine
- grated carrot and apple
- coleslaw
- sweetcorn, celery and ham
- smoked mackerel with orange segments.

Drinks:
- choose fruit juice or milk
- avoid too many sugary drinks and/or tea or coffee with sugar
- if you choose a soft drink make it sugar-free.

Scones and breads:
- plain scones, muffins or crumpets with a thin spread of jam
- also try fruit, currant, nut or seed bread.

Simple recipes – good to make when friends are round to study

For more substantial meals than the snacks given above, here are a few simple recipes which you can use for quick meals in the evening.

Pasta with tomato sauce

This is a great basic recipe which can form the base for lots of more complex meals. The quantities given here are for two people. The sauce will keep in the fridge for a day or two, and you can also freeze the sauce.

- 250g pasta (spaghetti or tagliatelle)
- 15ml oil (preferably olive oil, but sunflower oil works too)
- half an onion, finely sliced
- 1 garlic clove, chopped finely or crushed
- 400g can of chopped tomatoes
- salt and pepper
- 30g grated Parmesan cheese

Heat the oil gently in a frying pan. Chop the onion finely and fry in the oil with the crushed garlic until the onion is soft. Keep the heat down to stop the onion burning or browning. Add the tomatoes, salt and pepper, and heat through.

Cover the pan and allow the sauce to cook through for about 20 minutes – the tomatoes should break down into a pulp.

Cook the pasta according to the instructions on the packet. This should take about 10 minutes, so you can start this while the sauce is still cooking. Drain the pasta when it's cooked and put back in the pan you cooked it in. Add the sauce and stir together. Serve with a sprinkling of grated cheese on top.

If you want to add a bit of variety to this, try including some herbs in the sauce when you start cooking it. The usual ones are oregano and basil. You might be able to get fresh basil from your local supermarket. You can also add chopped grilled bacon to the sauce and you can also try different types of pasta, like penne, or conchiglia.

You can make a spicy version by adding chilli powder to the sauce, but be careful not to add too much. Try experimenting to find out just how hot you like it! Add some kidney beans to make a more substantial meal. Drain a small tin of kidney beans and wash them before adding them to the sauce.

Lemon-roasted chicken with sweet tomato pasta

The basic pasta with tomato sauce described above is used as a base for a really delicious chicken dish. The quantities below are for two people – it's too good to keep to yourself! It's a bit more time-consuming, because it involves making a marinade for the chicken and allowing the chicken to take in the flavours of the marinade.

- 1 lemon, zested and juiced
- 1 clove of garlic
- 1 small pinch mixed dried herbs
- 35ml olive oil
- salt and freshly ground black pepper
- 2 whole chicken legs
- 1 x quantity Tomato sauce and pasta

Zest the lemon by grating the yellow skin with a fine grater. Peel the garlic and crush with a garlic crusher. Put the garlic and lemon zest in a bowl and prepare the marinade by adding in the lemon juice, mixed herbs and olive oil, making sure it is all mixed well. Add salt and pepper and taste to check the seasoning.

Pour the marinade over the chicken legs, rubbing it into every nook and cranny. Cover and leave in the fridge for at least 2 hours, or preferably overnight so that the flavours can develop. You can cook the chicken straight away but the flavours will be nicer if you can leave it to marinate.

2

About an hour before you want to eat, preheat the oven to 200°C/gas 6, then transfer your chicken legs to a shallow baking tray. Spoon the marinade over the chicken legs and cook in the preheated oven for between 45 minutes to 1 hour, or until the chicken is golden, crisp and tender. While the chicken is cooking in the oven, prepare the pasta and tomato sauce, and serve the chicken with the juices and tomato pasta.

Chicken chow mein

Chow mein is a simple stir-fry which is very versatile, so once you've mastered the basics, you can make up your own variations.

- 100g dried Chinese noodles
- 60g chicken breast
- 1 tablespoon soy sauce
- 1 teaspoon sesame oil
- 1 tablespoon sunflower oil
- 1 garlic clove, chopped finely or crushed
- 15g mangetouts (or sugar snap peas)
- 3g beansprouts
- 15g ham, finely chopped
- 1 spring onion, finely chopped
- salt and pepper

Slice the chicken into fine strips. Put in a bowl and add about half the soy sauce and the sesame oil.

Cook the noodles in boiling water according to the instructions on the packet.

Heat half the sunflower oil in a wok or a deep frying pan over a high heat. Add the chicken mixture and stir-fry for 2-3 minutes. Transfer the chicken out of the wok onto a plate and keep it hot. Add the rest of the oil into the wok and heat it again, then stir in the mangetouts, beansprouts, ham and garlic for another minute or so, then add the cooked noodles.

Keep stir-frying the mixture till the noodles are heated through, then add the rest of the soy sauce and season with salt and pepper. Add the cooked chicken and the chopped spring onions, and give a final stir through before serving.

There are lots of variations to this dish. Instead of the chicken, you can use cooked prawns, or beef or pork. Other vegetables like sliced mushrooms, carrots or chopped baby sweetcorns can be used instead of the meat (or as well as the meat!).

Tuna and macaroni salad

This is a quick and easy salad with a full range of nutrition in one dish. As a bonus, it takes about as long to make the salad as it does to boil the water and cook the pasta. While the pasta cooks, prepare the remaining ingredients. Then, once the pasta has cooked, simply mix the ingredients together, taste and correct the seasonings and serve at room temperature or chill until ready to serve.

- 80g macaroni
- 1 tablespoon plain yoghurt
- 1 tablespoon mayonnaise
- 1 tablespoon lemon juice
- half a small onion, sliced finely
- half a stalk celery, diced small
- quarter of a red (or green or yellow) diced small pepper
- 1 tablespoon parsley, chopped
- 50g cheddar cheese, diced small
- 50g sweetcorn (defrosted or canned)
- pinch dried thyme, crumbled
- 80g tuna in water, drained
- salt and pepper to taste

Cook the macaroni according to the instructions on the packet.

While the pasta is cooking, place the yoghurt, mayonnaise and half of the lemon juice in a mixing bowl. Drain the pasta and pour it into the mixing bowl with some water still clinging to it. Stir the pasta, then add the onion, celery, pepper, parsley, cheese, corn and thyme. Stir in the tuna and remaining lemon juice, adding salt and pepper to taste. Taste the pasta and adjust the seasonings. Allow to cool and serve.

You can use other fish and seafood instead of the tuna, like smoked mackerel, salmon, or prawns, and you can use other vegetables like carrots and purple onions. And if you don't like any of the ingredients in the list, you can just leave them out and swap them for something you do like.

Top 10 brain booster foods

1 Oats/porridge good for slow release of energy for the brain.
2 Berries rich in antioxidants that protect the brain from pollution.
3 Boiled eggs contain phospholipids which enhance memory function in the brain.
4 Water helps hydration and increases concentration.
5 Apples, pears and apricots are good snacks to fuel the brain between meals as they release energy slowly.
6 Multigrain bread, nuts and seeds are high in vitamin B, which aids concentration and helps the nervous system.
7 Bananas contain potassium which aids memory recall.
8 Lean beef contains iron which helps concentration levels.
9 Salmon high in omega-3 oils needed to make brain cells.
10 Milk helps keep you alert as it contains protein which boosts levels of tyrosine, the brain-energising amino acid.

Drinking water

It's very easy to overlook the importance of drinking enough water during the day. Not drinking can affect concentration, bring on headaches and will reduce your energy levels. Drinking enough, or keeping properly hydrated, helps keep the body working properly, and if the body is working properly, there's a better chance the mind will work properly too. Doctors generally think it's important to take in between 1 and 2 litres of water every day, to replace what is lost through sweat and urine.

But it's important to drink the right amounts at the right times. If you drank 1 litre of water in one go, you'd feel bloated for a while and most of it would pass straight through without doing any good at all. So use this water diary as a guide to your water intake through the day, but remember – it is only a guide, and it's not too important if you don't stick to it exactly.

First thing in the morning
You lose a lot of water through sweat and breathing in the night, so it's important to replenish your supplies. A cup of hot water and a slice of lemon is a good way to start the day. Add a bit of honey for sweetness.

A glass of fruit juice at breakfast counts towards your intake of fluids. For a bit of variety, try adding some sparkling mineral water to give the juice some fizz.

Before you leave the house for school, it's a good idea to fill a bottle with water, and sip it on the bus or in the car.

Mid-morning
A cup of tea at morning break will keep the fluid levels up until lunchtime and will stop you feeling hungry during classes.

Lunchtime
It's actually better to have a glass of water before you eat your lunch than drinking it with lunch. Drinking water with a meal dilutes the digestive juices and makes it harder to digest food. You should also have a cup of tea or glass of juice after you've eaten, but wait for a while between eating and drinking.

Afternoon
If you go straight home after school, have a cup of tea or a glass of fruit juice when you get in. If you're staying at school for after-school activities, have a drink before you start, particularly if they're sporting activities. It's a good idea to have a protein-based snack to eat at this time too, to keep the blood-sugar levels up. Try a handful of nuts and raisins, for example.

Evening
Have a cup of tea or a glass of water after your evening meal, and then have a small glass about half an hour before you go to bed. Don't drink too much before bedtime, otherwise you'll have to get up during the night.

What to drink

As well as drinking enough at the right times, it's important to drink the right things. Tea, coffee and Coke™ all contain caffeine. Apart from keeping you awake, caffeine is a mild diuretic, which means it makes you urinate. So if you do have drinks with caffeine, remember that you do need a bit more liquid than if you have caffeine-free drinks. Remember too that caffeine is a stimulant, which can make stress worse, so it makes sense to try to keep your caffeine intake down if you want to reduce your stress levels.

Remember:
We are what we eat and drink. Give your body and your brain the best possible fuel.

CHOOSING YOUR WORKSPACE

Getting your workspace right is a crucial factor for you – where and how are you going to study?

You must bring in to play all that you have learnt from Chapter 1 about your learning style and preferences.

- Do you need quiet?
- Do you need a computer?
- Do you need music?
- Do you need friends to talk things over with?
- Do you have the correct equipment? Coloured pencils, highlighter pens, folders, polypockets.

Wherever you decide to study it is important that you:

- have a comfortable desk and chair and if you are a visual learner, keep away from visual distractions like windows.
- keep the room you are in at a comfortable temperature and good light – keep the reptilian brain happy.
- have the resources you need – paper, coloured pencils, highlighter pens, folders, polypockets, dividers, notes, e-mail and website addresses, dictionary, thesaurus and text books.
- have record cards, to write down important points (you'll read more about this in Chapter 3).
- have access to a computer to access websites that may assist you.
- are free from interruptions. Have your study timetable up in the kitchen, the loo or on your bedroom door to let everyone know when a good time to interrupt would be.
- avoid clutter in your environment, especially if you are left-brained. Keeping tidy also helps make sure you don't lose anything important.
- create a secure storage space for your study materials. This may be in you own bedroom, somewhere in the house, or a large plastic container if you share a bedroom.
- remember to have some treats about so you do not waste time going to the kitchen or to the shops.
- pace yourself. It is important to remember you are not alone – just think of how many pupils and students sitting exams around the country at this time.

- remember to develop high emotional intelligence – take time with family and friends.
- reward yourself and mark your progress so you can see what you have achieved.

Environment for a visual learner

- Do not sit beside or near a window – too tempting to day dream.
- Do not sit in a room with a TV on – you know you will watch it.

Environment for an audio learner

- Sit in a room where you can talk to yourself.
- Listen to yourself recite information on a tape recorder.
- Allow background music.
- Read aloud the information you are learning.

Environment for the kinaesthetic learner

- You have to be comfortable in your surroundings.
- Have space to move around.
- Have plenty of paper, pens and possibly a computer to make notes or mind-maps.
- See the section in Chapter 3 on learning with PowerPoint – this should suit you for essays.

Remember:
Take time to sort your place of study. Get it right for you.

INCREASING YOUR CONFIDENCE

This is the time when you need to believe in yourself and your own abilities. If you tell yourself you are not going to be able to do something or that you are going to fail, the chances are you will be right! The brain is an amazing organ but if you put in garbage it will put out garbage. How often have you said 'I CAN'T find my keys/wallet etc...' ? The truth is you might have difficulty finding them, but someone else comes along and says 'I WILL find your keys/wallet etc.... ' and lo and behold, they hold up the offending item, making you feel small and although you're relieved, you might be annoyed with yourself. Your reptilian brain was working overtime and you did not have the correct environment to think straight. Remember *flight and fright* in Chapter 1 – you had gone into panic mode. The person looking told their brain I WILL find so they programmed themselves for success.

Having confidence in yourself is vital to survive in the world. Examination time puts you under new pressures, but it's essential you keep your self-confidence. You must believe in your own abilities and strive to achieve your goals. There are always things which will knock our self-confidence, so we must work hard to develop it and nurture it so that it is healthy and renewable.

Tips for confidence

- Learn from past mistakes. Don't beat yourself up if you get something wrong – dwelling on failure is really 'self-pity'. Pick out the positive experiences, write them down, and use them to make a better experience. No mistake is going to be all bad – you will have learnt something you can use again, even if it is, for example, not to trust a certain person again!!!

- Write down what you would like to do as a sort of 'wish list'. Start to write down how you are going to achieve it. You will soon see that much of what you want is achievable with some effort.

- Do something different – challenge yourself. Take up a different sport or activity, meet new people, listen to new music. Surprise yourself at your own confidence. Most newcomers to an activity get a lot of help and advice, and you will probably be made to feel special and important.

- Work out your friendship grouping. Do some of your friends sap your confidence to help boost theirs? If they do, do you really want them as friends? If not, ditch them. Stick with people who are emotionally intelligent and try to make you feel good about yourself.

- Know your own strengths – write a list of them and keep it up on a wall or in a journal and refer to them when you are low. This will help to focus on the positive.
- Take responsibility and make sure you are in control of situations.
- Have positive 'self-talk', make up positive mantras like 'I will pass my next exam'.
- Make a list of what worries and annoys you, then write down how you would handle them if they occurred. This gives you more control when they do happen. Mental preparation is like a rehearsal of the situation, with you getting what you want out of it.
- Try to be focussed on solutions to a problem. If you're in a difficult situation, stick with it to make it work instead of giving up. People admire the person who can salvage the situation. Use your initiative.
- Walk tall and confident. Hold eye contact with who you are talking with when they are talking to you.

Beat exam stress

During the period that you are revising, you may experience some stress and fatigue. If you notice you are always tired, irritable, without much of an appetite, or simply feeling run down, it is important that you try to reduce the stress levels and get back on track.

It is crucial to take on board the health section in this chapter to keep you at your optimum fitness levels to achieve success in the examinations.

- Exercise to rid the body of excess adrenaline.
- Sleep at least eight hours a day.
- Eat a variety of foods to help improve memory and curb mood swings.

Relaxation techniques

BEFORE SLEEP

1 Take time to clear your mind of anxiety. Play some quiet soothing music and sit or lie comfortably, blocking out any other thoughts other than calming yourself and focus on just you and your breathing. Breathe deeply and slowly for ten breaths. Then breathe normally until you feel totally relaxed.

BEFORE THE EXAMINATION

2 Sit up straight, close your eyes and breathe out until you empty your lungs. Hold for three seconds, then breathe slowly until you feel your lungs full again. Repeat this exercise until you feel calm and in control.

Perform well in the examination

- Show a confident, organised approach to your answers.
- Keep your work tidy.
- Show your intentions with a plan/map of your answer.
- Write legibly and neatly.
- Use headings, number answers, and label diagrams.
- Leave space between answers, in case you go back and put in more detail, later on, when rereading your work.

Know where to go for help

If you are experiencing problems that this book has not covered, it is essential you seek help. Always remember that if you need help or have a problem it's better to ask for help than just letting it linger on. It may be a parent or a teacher or lecturer who can help, or it may be more specialist help that is required. Here are a few support services:

- Panic attack
  Information and self help techniques.
  http://www.panic-attacks.co.uk/index.htm
- Basic relaxation exercises
  http://www.bbc.co.uk/health/mental/copingrelaxation.shtml
- Samaritans
  http://www.samaritans.org.uk/
  tel: 08457 90 90 90
- Childline
  http://www.childline.org.uk/
  tel: 0800 1111
- Children's Legal Centre
  http://www.childrenslegalcentre.com/
- Anti-bullying Campaign
  http://www.bullying.co.uk/

Remember:
Believe in yourself. You are very special. If you ever find yourself questioning that, there are ways of removing the doubts. Don't give them any room in your mind. Get rid of them.

CHAPTER SUMMARY

What's In It For Me!

As a nation we have a dreadful reputation for leading unhealthy lives. Follow the advice in this chapter and you will:

■   feel better about yourself

■   be better equipped to study and then sit your exams

■   have more energy for all the other things you want to do

■   improve your prospects for living longer and more happily.

Why should you settle for being less that you could be, when a few simple changes in your lifestyle could transform the person you are.

ELSIE INGLIS

Elsie Inglis was born in India in 1864 at a time when women were not allowed to vote and rarely got to study at university. Elsie came to Scotland as a child and, as she grew up, became determined to change things for women.

Elsie worked hard, she was clever and she was not prepared to let the prejudices of the day hold her back from doing good in the world. She got the qualifications needed to go to university and was admitted to medical school – very unusual at the time. She specialised in surgery but, after qualifying, she found it difficult to practise her profession because male doctors would not take her seriously.

Undeterred she set up her own maternity hospital in Edinburgh in 1901. This became the famous Elsie Inglis Memorial Maternity hospital and it was staffed entirely by women. Elsie also became involved politically in the campaign for women's suffrage and in 1906 she founded the Scottish Women's Suffrage Federation. She campaigned tirelessly for the next eight years to win votes for women. But then came the First World War.

Elsie wanted to take her medical skills to the front line but once again was prevented from doing so because she was a woman. She and the Federation formed women-only medical units. The first was sent to France, the second to the Serbian front. Elsie went with the Serbian unit.

Conditions were appalling but Elsie and her female medics endured the cold, the poor food, the lack of sanitation and inadequate clothing along with the soldiers. She was captured by the Austrians, freed, but then returned to the front. But now her own health was damaged beyond recovery. She was sent back home and died on the very day her ship sailed into Newcastle. She was buried in Edinburgh.

Winston Churchill said that Elsie and her example would never be forgotten. A Russian who saw Elsie and her team in Serbia believed Britain would always be a great nation if it produced people like Elsie. Some historians believe that the much more famous Florence Nightingale had achieved nothing like as much as Elsie.

The lesson: All of us find there are obstacles in life. We can go round them, over them, under them or we can smash them down. It is important not just to give up when the going gets hard. Elsie didn't.

STUDY TECHNIQUES

Studying is about reading, taking notes and doing practice exam questions. In this chapter you will find advice on how to:

- Read so that you can extract from a book or set of printed notes the information that you need.
- Make your own notes so that you remember what you have read.
- Tackle past exam papers so that you become more confident about sitting your own exams.

READING

Everyone can read more effectively if they practise some simple techniques. These can seem a little strange or difficult to begin with, but you will quickly get the hang of it. After all, athletes have to train for their events; apprentices have to learn the skills of the job. If you are reading this book, you are almost certainly in training – for your exams; and you have to master a key skill – study reading. This means:

1 Concentrating
2 reading with a purpose
3 using (and not being scared of) books – skimming, gutting, reinforcing
4 reading with a pencil.

Concentrating

Concentration means that you are devoting your whole mind to the task in hand. You are focussed and you are not thinking about other things. Serious concentration does not come easily. Sometimes you can see athletes making huge efforts to stay concentrated, pacing around before a big race, blotting out all distractions; you see tennis players narrowing their eyes, staring intently at the ball; you notice football defenders keeping their discipline and not letting the striker find a space between them. But, during a long tennis match or 90 minutes of football, you also see the concentration breaking, a mistake being made and a point or goal being lost.

There is a lesson for students in this. *Intense concentration is almost impossible to sustain for a long period of time.*

How often have you read a page of a book and, at the end of it, had no idea what you have just read? Studying should therefore take place in short bursts of 30 to 40 minutes maximum. With practice, you should be able to retain focus for this length of time. If you work for longer your mind will inevitably wander, unless you are a quite exceptional individual. After 40 minutes, therefore, you should take a break of five to ten minutes and then you can start another 40 minute session.

It is amazing how much you can read and how much you can learn if you do not let yourself get distracted. Getting it right first time saves you time (and gives you more revision time) because it means you don't have to go back over the same pages over and over again.

So, when you get down to serious reading, you have to find a room where you will not be distracted. Some music might help you work, but television and other people talking will most definitely not. Forty minutes concentrated reading should mean just that and nothing else.

You could, for example, use the break after the 40 minute session to send a text and definitely to have a glass of water (see Chapter 2). But then you must quickly get your focus back to do another 40 minute session.

Remember:
Read in 40 minute bursts of intense concentration in an environment where you will not be distracted.

Reading with a purpose

Much time can be wasted when your reading lacks purpose. You know you should be reading and probably that means the book is in front of you. But why? To what end? Are you sure you know what the point of the reading is?

- Are you trying to get an overview of a topic?
- Are you wanting to find out and then remember specific facts?
- Are you seeking to reinforce what you already know?
- Are you looking for a new perspective or viewpoint on a familiar subject?
- Are you collecting information for an essay answer?

and so on.

You will study much more effectively if, before you start reading a book or set of notes, you are very clear about what you are trying to find out.

Study reading is not the same as reading a book on the beach. Picking up a thriller, such as *The Da Vinci Code*, during the summer holidays is about entertainment. But study reading is not about entertainment. You may well find your study reading very uninteresting at first, and it might not be easy to understand.

But the more you learn about a subject, the more fascinating it can become. It is a very good tactic to insist to yourself that what you are revising really does interest you. Convince yourself of this and you will transform your studies.

Remember: Read with a purpose; know before you start what you want to get out of a book.

If you still find the reading really difficult, try focussing on the *What's in it for me?* factor. Better study reading means better grades and not having to worry about the results envelope popping through your door in August!

Using (and not being scared of) books – skimming, gutting, reinforcing

Remember that non-fiction books are meant to be used. Take out of them what you need but do not feel that you have to read everything, unlike a novel.

Do not be put off by the number of pages. It is easy to be scared by a book that looks so large that you believe you could never read it. But, among the 800 pages that appear so frightening, it may be that there are only ten pages that cover the information you are seeking. It is these ten pages that you will read and you can ignore the other 790.

If it is a set of handout notes you are reading, do make sure that you have them all and that they are in the right order. Many Standard and Higher Grade candidates are far too casual with the printed sheets that their teachers give them. Many of these notes will have been specially tailored to the course and will therefore richly reward careful reading. But it is definitely your responsibility to ensure that you have them all and that they are in a fit state for close reading.

> **Remember:**
> Do not be intimidated by books. They are there to be used. Ensure that you have a full set of handout notes.

How then should you read a book for information?

Get a feel for the book
Before you start reading, pick up the book in question and get a feel for it. Look at the chapter headings, check if it has an index, see if it has any helpful diagrams and maps, decide if it is definitely a book that is appropriate for you.

Skim read a chapter
Select the first chapter that seems to be relevant to your purposes and read it very quickly. Sweep your eyes across the pages. You will notice words associated with the topic you are studying. Read the first and last paragraphs in the chapter more carefully. Note the first and last sentences in other paragraphs. You can cover 20 pages in five minutes doing this skim reading. You will get an overview of what you will later read more carefully. You will pick up how the chapter has been constructed and that will help you put together your own notes.

Gut the chapter
Now comes the hard work. You must now go back through the chapter a second time, much more slowly. Read the relevant bits carefully, ensuring that you understand everything the author is explaining and asking yourself whether you agree with them when they are arguing a point of view. Keep a pencil in your hand and take notes (see next page).

Reinforce what you have learned

When you have finished gutting the chapter, skim read it again. The few minutes spent on this 'warming down' exercise are vitally important. They fix in your mind what you have been reading and they provide a quick check on whether you have missed something important.

> Remember: Skim, gut, reinforce.

Reading with a pencil

A final tip on reading. In order to maintain the concentration discussed earlier, read with a pencil in your hand.

A pencil can help your eyes follow text. Run it down the page as you read. Do not be embarrassed to do this, just because little children point to words when they are learning to read. The fastest readers in the world use this technique to help their concentration.

You should also try to read actively, rather than passively. Engage with the book. The easiest way to do this is have a pencil in your hand and take notes as you read. This is demanding! It means thinking for yourself, and actually doing something, as opposed to just letting the words wash over you. But you have to do it. Reading with a pencil to take notes helps retain focus, makes your reading more efficient, and helps you to remember what you have been reading.

> Remember: A pencil will improve your reading and help you recall what you have learned.

NOTE-TAKING

Note-taking is at the heart of good studying. It is important to spend a bit of time learning this very important skill, practising different approaches and finding out what suits you best.

The section which follows will make some suggestions on how to take notes. If you have time, try them all and decide which you like. Even better, develop your own style of note-taking which might be a combination of what follows. But do take notes and do use the style which works for you, as you move into your period of most intense study.

Consider this passage of text about Winston Churchill. It is only an example. It could have been about some aspect of science or English literature or sporting technique. It happens to be about the early life of Winston Churchill and we must imagine that our purpose is to find out some key biographical details about the Prime Minister who led us to victory in World War Two.

The Early Life of Winston Churchill

Winston Churchill was the eldest son of the Lord Randolph Churchill and Jennie Jerome. He was born prematurely on November 30 1874 at Blenheim Palace in Oxfordshire and was christened Winston Leonard Spencer Churchill. His father was a noted Tory politician who was descended from John Churchill, 1st Duke of Marlborough, the hero of the wars against Louis XIV of France in the early 18th century. His mother, a noted society beauty, was the daughter of a New York financier and horse-racing enthusiast, Leonard W. Jerome.

As a child, Churchill and his younger brother Jack were cared for by their devoted nurse Mrs Everest. Despite her affection, he was neglected by his parents and did not have a happy childhood. He was sent to Harrow School, but despite a growing interest in literature and writing, his academic record was poor, justifying his father's decision to enter him into an army career. He passed the entrance examination to the Royal Military College, Sandhurst, at his third attempt. He worked hard and passed out 20th in a class of 130 in 1894.

In 1895, after leaving Sandhurst, he was appointed a second lieutenant in the Fourth Queen's Own Hussars cavalry regiment a month after his father's death. His first posting was as a military observer in Cuba, gathering information on the Spanish-Cuban-American war, and it was here that his journalistic interests began, reporting on the war for the London Daily Graphic.

His regiment went to India in 1896, where he saw service as both soldier and journalist on the North-West Frontier. His dispatches were published successfully in 1898 as The Story of the Malakand Field Force, launching his career as a writer. He was then attached to Lord Kitchener's Nile expeditionary force in the same dual role of soldier and correspondent, again publishing his dispatches, The River War. His first and only novel Savrola was published in 1900.

Skim over the passage. Take about five seconds to do that. It is immediately obvious that we have got something useful here. It is about Churchill's early life and it clearly contains a lot of factual information that will be useful to us. Our challenge now is to read it carefully (really concentrating) and to take notes which will help us to remember the key facts.

Highlighting

If the passage is from a book we own, or if it is a photocopied sheet that we can write on, then we could mark the passage using a highlighter pen, as below:

The Early Life of Winston Churchill

Winston Churchill was the eldest son of the Lord Randolph Churchill and Jennie Jerome. He was born prematurely on November 30 1874 at Blenheim Palace in Oxfordshire and was christened Winston Leonard Spencer Churchill. His father was a noted Tory politician who was descended from John Churchill, 1st Duke of Marlborough, the hero of the wars against Louis XIV of France in the early 18th century. His mother, a noted society beauty, was the daughter of a New York financier and horse-racing enthusiast, Leonard W. Jerome.

As a child, Churchill and his younger brother Jack were cared for by their devoted nurse Mrs Everest. Despite her affection, he was neglected by his parents and did not have a happy childhood. He was sent to Harrow School, but despite a growing interest in literature and writing, his academic record was poor, justifying his father's decision to enter him into an army career. He passed the entrance examination to the Royal Military College, Sandhurst, at his third attempt. He worked hard and passed out 20th in a class of 130 in 1894.

In 1895, after leaving Sandhurst, he was appointed a second lieutenant in the Fourth Queen's Own Hussars cavalry regiment a month after his father's death. His first posting was as a military observer in Cuba, gathering information on the Spanish-Cuban-American war, and it was here that his journalistic interests began, reporting on the war for the London Daily Graphic.

His regiment went to India in 1896, where he saw service as both soldier and journalist on the North-West Frontier. His dispatches were published successfully in 1898 as The Story of the Malakand Field Force, launching his career as a writer. He was then attached to Lord Kitchener's Nile expeditionary force in the same dual role of soldier and correspondent, again publishing his dispatches, The River War. His first and only novel Savrola was published in 1900.

Using a highlighter pen in this way has become popular with students in recent years and it can be very effective. It is a modern version of underlining key words and lines. There is a danger, however. It is so easy to use a highlighter pen that one can get carried away and highlight too much. There are school notes where almost the whole page looks to be covered in fluorescent ink. Where then are the highlights? Especially if you already have the sheet or book, what is gaining by turning the text yellow, if it does not actually identify the key points. This criticism, though, is not to distract from the value of the highlighter pen. But, if you are using one, do not overuse it.

Margin marking

Margin marking is a technique which involves marking key passages with a small pencil line in the left-hand margin on a first reading of the passage. On reading it for a second time, a double line can be placed in the right-hand margin, but only against those bits that now seem more than just important; you now know that they are absolutely crucial.

The Early Life of Winston Churchill

Winston Churchill was the eldest son of the Lord Randolph Churchill and Jennie Jerome. He was born prematurely on November 30 1874 at Blenheim Palace in Oxfordshire and was christened Winston Leonard Spencer Churchill. His father was a noted Tory politician who was descended from John Churchill, 1st Duke of Marlborough, the hero of the wars against Louis XIV of France in the early 18th century. His mother, a noted society beauty, was the daughter of a New York financier and horse-racing enthusiast, Leonard W. Jerome.

As a child, Churchill and his younger brother Jack were cared for by their devoted nurse Mrs Everest. Despite her affection, he was neglected by his parents and did not have a happy childhood. He was sent to Harrow School, but despite a growing interest in literature and writing, his academic record was poor, justifying his father's decision to enter him into an army career. He passed the entrance examination to the Royal Military College, Sandhurst, at his third attempt. He worked hard and passed out 20th in a class of 130 in 1894.

In 1895, after leaving Sandhurst, he was appointed a second lieutenant in the Fourth Queen's Own Hussars cavalry regiment a month after his father's death. His first posting was as a military observer in Cuba, gathering information on the Spanish-Cuban-American war, and it was here that his journalistic interests began, reporting on the war for the London Daily Graphic.

His regiment went to India in 1896, where he saw service as both soldier and journalist on the North-West Frontier. His dispatches were published successfully in 1898 as The Story of the Malakand Field Force, launching his career as a writer. He was then attached to Lord Kitchener's Nile expeditionary force in the same dual role of soldier and correspondent, again publishing his dispatches, The River War. His first and only novel Savrola was published in 1900.

In the immediate run-up to the exam with time running short, you can quickly read the book or passage by glancing, not at the whole text, but just at those bits marked with a single line in the left-hand margin. The night before, even the hour before the exam, the passage can be given a final check by simply reading the double lines in the right-hand margin.

What to do when the book is not yours

But, if the book is not yours, you must not write on it. You will need to get a notepad and write your notes in that. There are some golden rules here which you must not forget:

- Always take a careful note of the book title, its author, its date of publication and the page number that your note is coming from. This is information you might need later.
- Do not copy out whole sentences unless they are actual, direct quotes, which you might want to use. Develop you own shorthand notations to speed yourself up.
- Do not be tempted to start writing detailed notes during the skim reading stage (see above). To do so is to run the risk of missing the wood for trees and of writing down far more than is necessary.

Headings, sub-headings and bullet points

An excellent approach to writing your own notes is to use bullet points gathered under headings, as in this example, still based on the Churchill passage.

The Early Life of Winston Churchill

BIRTH
- 1874
- at Blenheim
- parents: Randolph and Jennie.

CHILDHOOD AND EDUCATION
- Mrs Everest, nanny
- neglected by parents
- Harrow
- poor academic record.

FIRST CAREER: SOLDIER
- Sandhurst (3rd attempt)
- became more serious
- 20/130
- India
- Kitchener's Nile expedition.

SECOND CAREER: WRITER AND JOURNALIST
- Daily Graphic
- Malakand Field Force (India)
- River War (Nile)
- Savrola (novel).

If, in the gutting stage of your reading, you have read carefully and understood the main aspects of Churchill's early life, then the above notes should be enough to bring the story back into your mind and allow you to write your own paragraph about this period in Churchill's famous career.

Using a computer

Most schools nowadays can provide pupils with access to computers and many homes have their own. They are excellent for note-taking. They can be used in a whole host of ways, but perhaps the most common will be finding information on the internet, making notes and writing essays.

If you use your computer to seek out information on the internet, be careful with the information you find on the Web. Some of it is very biased and some of it is complete rubbish. Before you start taking notes, check that the website you are using is reliable and reputable.

One really excellent address for Standard Grade and Higher candidates is **http://www.leckieandleckie.co.uk/** where you will find the Leckie & Leckie Revision Guides. These are an invaluable revision resource. Most subjects are covered with summary notes already prepared for you.

Create notes in electronic form

Any word processor will allow you to type up information in the form of bullet points, but have you ever considered using PowerPoint? This well-known program is very popular for presentation purposes. Many teachers like to use it in their lessons. However, it is also good for note-taking. Here is what you do.

Put each fact or idea that you want to remember (the bits of the passage you might have underlined or noted as a series of bullet points or put on a mind-map) onto a new slide. So, for Churchill's early life you could have created this slide:

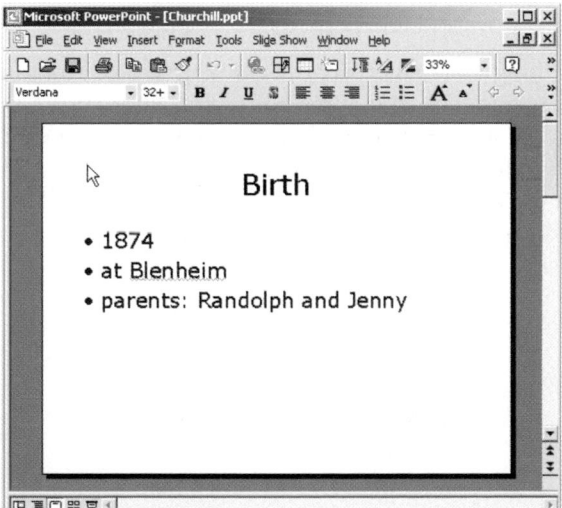

Other slides might contain facts about Churchill's parents, birthplace, school, etc. Once you have noted all the key facts and quotations that you need, and created all the necessary slides, you can do two things. First you can look at the slide sorter view.

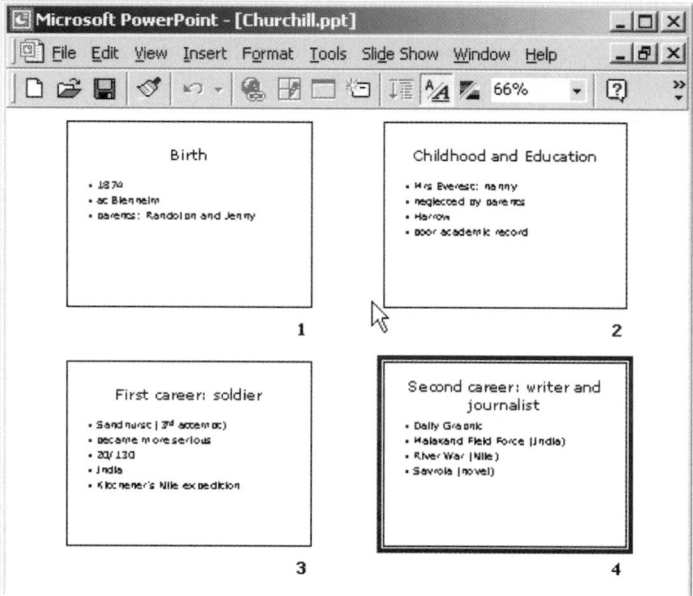

This is a very helpful PowerPoint mode. It gives you an overview of all your notes and enables you to move your slides around, putting the facts in the order you want them, perhaps for writing an essay.

The second thing you can do is print off your slides. You can set PowerPoint to give you two, three, four or six slides per A4 page. It is easy then to cut up the slides and use them as reminder cards. You can test yourself with these or get someone else to ask you questions from them. With the following three-slide example, you could cover up the left-hand side and try to write down from memory the key points on the right-hand side.

Birth

- 1874
- at Blenheim
- parents: Randolph and Jennie

_____

_____

_____

_____

Childhood and Education

- Mrs Everest: nanny
- neglected by parents
- Harrow
- poor academic record

Second career: writer and journalist

- Daily Graphic
- Malakand Field Force (India)
- River War (Nile)
- Savrola (novel)

First career: soldier

- Sandhurst (3rd attempt)
- became more serious
- 20/130
- India
- Kitchener's Nile expedition

Of course, if you ever want to add to your notes, it is easy to go back to your PowerPoint file and create extra slides.

You might also run your slides onscreen as a slide show with each point being displayed in turn. You can try to recall what the point should be, before clicking the mouse to find out what it actually is. This is a very easy way of testing yourself.

If you are not familiar with PowerPoint, think seriously about learning how to use it. It is not difficult. With a little bit of help, you will be putting your own document together in half an hour.

Using mind-maps

Mind-maps have grown greatly in popularity in recent years. They are particularly associated with the writer and lecturer Tony Buzan who claims that using mind-maps can greatly improve academic performance. There are references to his work in the Further Reading section at the end of this book.

To create a mind-map, take a blank sheet of paper and turn it sideways (landscape). Put the main title of your note in the middle, as below:

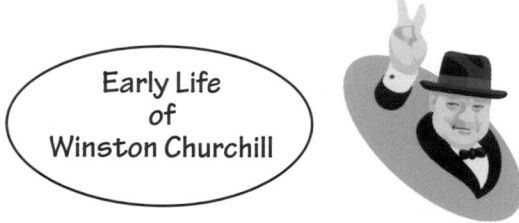

Draw main branches out from the title and write on them your main subheadings. Create smaller branches and write on them the information that you might have underlined or recorded as bullet points in other forms of note-taking.

Below you can see how the paragraph about Churchill's early life has been converted into a mind-map. Note the use of colour and of pictures (easily obtained from the Web). These help to personalise the map and make it more memorable. That makes the information easier to recall.

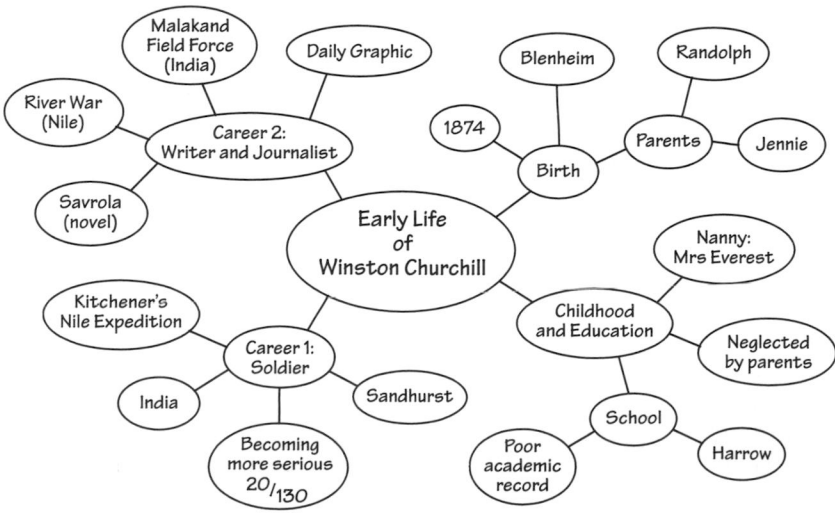

You should try drawing a few mind-maps. You might find that they suit your style of learning perfectly. But, even if you decide that mind-mapping is not your preferred method of studying and revising, you will still find that the very act of creating a map will help you to understand what you have been reading and to recall the important facts and ideas.

You would also be well advised to have a look online at 3MRT.com. This is an internet company which has produced mind-map versions of all the Standard grade and Higher grade Leckie & Leckie revision textbooks. The software allows you to test yourself and to compare your progress with other exam candidates who are also working online. It permits you to customise the maps to suit yourself. It is a very powerful revision tool for Scottish exam candidates, exciting and highly recommended. Details on how to access 3MRT are contained in the Further Reading section.

REMEMBERING

The most important key to remembering is to understand the topic in the first place. Keep rereading, keep asking the teacher, keep trying questions until you are sure you understand the subject. Build up your own set of notes, as detailed above, and they will reinforce your knowledge. Revise regularly and that will ensure the knowledge is embedded deep in your long-term memory.

Once you're sure you understand the subject, have confidence in yourself. Believe that you know something and that you are not going to forget it.

You can train your memory by 'exercising' it every day. Be organised: don't forget your PE kit or the message you were asked to deliver or to set the video recorder for the programme you don't want to miss. A fit memory will help you with day-to-day living and it will also make all the difference to your studying. Here are some simple memory tricks which you might find useful.

Put it in your way
If you have to take something with you in the morning, put it in front of your bedroom door before you go to bed, so it's in your way when you leave your room in the morning.

Bands and pins
Some people use a rubber band round their wrist to remind them to do

something. Anything unusual can be a reminder, like a band or a safety pin pinned to your bag.

Notices

Simple – write a note to yourself and stick it somewhere where you are bound to see it, like the front door, or the bathroom mirror!

Move things

Sometimes you'll think of things you need to do last thing at night just as you're going to sleep. If you're worried you'll forget, try changing something around you in bed, like the position of your bedside light, or throw a pillow on the floor where you'll see it in the morning. When you wake up in the morning, you'll see something different and gradually remember what you were thinking about.

Habits

If you need to do something regularly, associate it with something else you also need to do regularly. For example, if you need to take tablets in the morning, tape the bottle to your breakfast cereal so that you're bound to notice them.

Change your watch

If you wear a watch, swap it from one wrist to the other. When you look to see the time, you'll be reminded that there's something you need to remember.

DOING PAST PAPERS

If you are serious about passing exams, then nothing is more important than doing past papers. If you take nothing else from this book, do take this advice. The most productive studying you can possibly do is going over past papers.

What do Examiners want?

Examiners, and everyone else, want you to do well. Question setters are not in the business of making up impossible exams for the average candidate; nor do they want deliberately to trip you up. They *may* want to make you think but that is another matter.

What questions are likely to be asked?

Course syllabuses don't usually change much from one year to the next. When they do, the changes are clearly highlighted and lots of example questions are provided. In most courses there are certain topics which are more important than others and are so crucial that the subject would be virtually meaningless if they were to be missed out.

Consider a Maths syllabus, for example, which emphasises the solving of quadratic equations, or an English course which has Macbeth as the set Shakespearian text, or a modern History course which covers the Twentieth Century and which begins with the Treaty of Versailles. In each of these cases, the topics mentioned are just so vital that they cannot be missed out of the final exam. If they were, the exam would be a distortion of what the course was about and would not be testing whether the student has properly understood the subject. There *has* to be a question involving the solution of a quadratic function, somewhere there *has* to be the opportunity to write about Macbeth, and the Treaty of Versailles *must* feature in one guise or another in the respective exams for the Maths, English and History courses described above.

Such questions are known as 'bankers'. If you do not know what these questions are and if you haven't fully revised the bankers for the subjects you are studying, then you are not preparing yourself properly.

Why is doing past papers important?

- It is the easiest way to identify the 'bankers'. Sometimes you have to read questions a few times before you recognise exactly what they are asking. You can be sure the bankers will be there somewhere.
- It will convince you that the teacher is giving you good advice and should be listened to.
- It gives you the opportunity to practise. Athletes train for the big event; actors rehearse before the play goes live; musicians try out their ideas many times before they make a CD; and good candidates must practise questions before they enter the hall to sit their final exam.

How do I obtain past papers?

Past papers can often be obtained from your teacher or in the school library. Indeed your teacher will probably set past questions for you to tackle in class or for homework. You would be well advised to do these very conscientiously.

In the case of SQA examinations, past papers are collected and published by Leckie & Leckie and are available in most good bookshops. They are an excellent buy. Get the most up-to-date versions and get them for all the subjects you are studying. If the bookshop doesn't have the ones you need in stock, ask the shop to order them. That will cost you quite a few pounds but it will be a very good investment. And later you will probably be able to sell them on to an exam candidate in the year behind you.

If you can do all the questions that have been asked for a subject over, say, the last three years, you will not fail the actual exam that you have to sit. So carefully read through all the previous questions relevant to the syllabus you have been studying.

You should practise in several ways.

Make sure you know what questions you should be able to do!
Bear in mind that there is usually more than one way through a syllabus and that many syllabuses cannot be covered in their entirety in the time available. Your teacher will have chosen a particular route through the course, emphasising certain topics, spending less time on other aspects and leaving out some parts of the syllabus altogether.

Your teacher will almost certainly explain which parts of the syllabus have been covered and why those sections were chosen. If you're not sure about the syllabus, or if you have any other questions, don't be afraid to ask your teacher again. It's very important that you get this clear in your mind. This is too important to avoid asking a question in case you look foolish. Perhaps you will look foolish for a few moments; you will look a lot more foolish come the exam day if you haven't got this vital matter sorted out.

Become familiar with the questions
Read each question very carefully. Check you know *exactly* what the question is asking you to do. This is crucial. Every word in the question matters. You should get to know the 'vocabulary' of questions. Opposite is a list of terms taken from the SQA website. This is how the examiners expect you to interpret questions.

Key words	What does it mean?	How should it be answered?
Analyse	Consider, evaluate, examine in detail.	Give an account that is detailed using the factors that are to be analysed. Support any findings with examples where possible.
Compare, Distinguish	Demonstrate knowledge and understanding of both the similarities and differences between methods/choices.	Point out similarities and differences and perhaps reach a conclusion about which is preferable.
Contrast	Set in opposition in order to bring out the differences.	Draw up a distinction between the options.
Criticise	Analyse and then make a judgement or give an opinion.	Give your judgement about the merit of opinions or about the truth of facts and back up judgement by a discussion of the evidence or the reasoning involved.
Define	Set down the precise meaning of a word, phrase or concept.	Give the meaning. This should be short.
Discuss	Debate, examine, confer, talk about, deliberate – produce evidence of a development.	Investigate or examine by argument: sift and debate: give reasons for and against. Also examine the implications.
Describe	Give a detailed account of. Explain/illustrate/express.	Definition and/or explanation should be given.
Evaluate	State the positive and negative points. Attempt to justify your answer with expert opinion.	Analyse – make an appraisal of the worth of something or of some situation in the light of its truth or usefulness.
Explain	Make plain; interpret and account for; give reasons for.	Explain the option(s) and what it does/how it works/the effects.
Illustrate Interpret	Make clear and explicit.	Show by explaining and examples. Explain the meaning by giving opinions.
Justify	Give explanation for. Rationalise. Give good reasons for.	Show adequate grounds for decisions or conclusions; answer the main objections likely to be made to them. State why a course of action or option has been chosen.
Outline	Summarise – description without too much detail.	Give the main features or general principles of a subject omitting minor details and emphasising structure.
Relate or narrate	Communicate ideas and information on a subject.	Show how things are connected to each other, and to what extent they are alike or affect each other.
State	Present in brief, clear form.	Reasons for a particular option or course of action.
Summarise	Give the main points of an idea or argument.	Give a concise account of the chief points of a matter, omitting details and examples.

Work through questions

Do questions in your head, perhaps jotting down a few notes as you work your way through them. In Maths or Physics, for example, you could note the formulae you would employ; in English and History you could list the key dates, personalities, paragraph headings that you would work with if you were writing out the answer.

- Identify the questions, or bits of questions that you cannot do. Return to your course notes or your textbook and find out the method or the information you need in order to do them. Then go back and tackle the questions again.

- Speak to your teacher if you still cannot do the question. Don't be shy about this. Once again, this is too important to be held back by shyness. Tell your teacher or tutor where you are stuck and get him or her to show you how to do the question. Then tackle it again on your own.

- Never abandon a question as impossible. Keep at it until you can do it. When you finally crack it, you will hugely increase your self-confidence. You will be less intimidated by the difficult question which you are bound to come across in the real exam when you finally sit it.

Learn how to time answers

It will always repay you to produce a balanced answer paper. Four essays of roughly equal length will always do better than three longer essays and a couple of lines for the fourth. Self-discipline is required here in order to be restrained on the answer you know a lot about and to spend an equal amount of time on the one you are less sure of.

You should therefore work out how long to spend on an answer in each of your exams. This is not simply a matter of taking the total number of minutes allocated to the whole exam and dividing them by the number of marks the paper is worth. Before you do that piece of arithmetic, you should knock some time off for reading the exam paper and for deciding and planning the questions you are going to answer. You should also leave some minutes for reading over your answers at the end, before you hand in your paper. For a 150 minute exam, therefore, you should probably deduct up to 15 minutes for these activities.

But then you can calculate how many minutes to spend on each mark in the exam. Clearly you should be spending longer on a ten mark question than on a two mark question.

When doing exams, it is a good idea to have a watch on your desk beside you. As mentioned above, many candidates do less well than they might, because they do not work in an even-paced way through their exams. It is therefore well worth practising against the clock.

Do an exam paper against the clock

You will notice that we are not recommending you do all the past papers under exam conditions. It would be wonderful if you did, but you must be realistic. Most students will find that there is not the time to write out full answers for all the past papers. That is why it is suggested that you do every question *in your head*, jotting down only a few notes. In doing this you must be honest with yourself. Be sure, as you work through the question in your mind, that you really do know what you are doing and that you definitely could write it all down if you had to.

And every now and then, you must try a whole paper! Set an evening aside, sit down where you will not be disturbed and where the room is as much like exam conditions as you can make it. Open a past paper and do it without reference to any notes and within the time limit set for the exam. If it is a two hour exam, then two hours is what you must give yourself and not a minute more. Most teachers will be happy to look over what you produce in this situation and will perhaps give you a mark and help you with any difficulties you encountered.

Do questions and bits of questions against the clock

Even doing the whole of just one past paper for each of your subjects will prove very time consuming. Is there anything else that can be done to get essential exam practice? Yes there is – and that is to do single questions against the stopwatch. Here is what you should do.

Assuming you have worked out how much time you should spend on each mark, as described above, you can time yourself doing questions and even bits of questions from past papers. If, for example, you know you should spend a minute per mark, then you can try doing a ten mark question in a strict ten minutes. If after ten minutes your answer is unsatisfactory, try it again until you are satisfied both with what you are writing and with your timing.

Practice of this sort will help you:

- pick up a rhythm for each exam
- get a feel for what the examiners are likely to ask
- know in yourself that you are getting better.

You might even find yourself looking forward to the real thing, your cup final, your Olympic race. Be confident that you will be a winner.

CHAPTER SUMMARY

What's In It For Me!

Reading is at the heart of studying. You will study more efficiently, remember information better and have greater success in your exams if you:

- read with concentration and purpose
- study in bursts of about 40 minutes
- skim, gut and reinforce
- take notes in a format that suits you
- do past papers.

Studying requires hard work, sacrifice and commitment. But do it well and conscientiously and you will find yourself enjoying subjects and gaining great personal satisfaction. You will be vastly improving your chances of exam success.

DAVID LIVINGSTONE

David Livingstone was an astonishing man. He is remembered as a great nineteenth century explorer and missionary. His journeys required tremendous physical resilience as he fought against difficult terrain, burning heat and debilitating diseases, and there was also the ever-present danger of attack from hostile natives and wild animals. On one occasion he was actually mauled by a lion and lived to tell the tale.

A newspaper famously sent Henry Stanley to Africa to 'find' Livingstone. As far as Livingstone was concerned, he had never been lost but when Stanley eventually entered his camp, he greeted Livingstone with the famous lines, 'Dr Livingstone, I presume.' Livingstone did not return with Stanley to Europe but stayed on in Africa until his death when two young men who had been his close companions carried his body hundreds of miles to the coast so that it could be returned to Britain. He was a major campaigner against the evils of the slave trade and the people he fought to free never forgot him.

In all of this it must be remembered that Livingstone had no advantages when he was growing up in Blantyre, near Hamilton. He had to work during the day in a local mill, but he was determined to get an education. Sometimes he propped a book up against his machine. Often he sat up late at night reading by moonlight. It was never easy for him, but he never gave up. He wanted to be a minister but the first time he stood in the pulpit of a church to preach a sermon, he forgot everything he was going to say. He said in front of everyone that he could not remember a thing and then he walked out of the church, past an astonished congregation. It must have been hugely embarrassing for him at the time, but he refused to let it put him off his chosen career.

The lesson: Even great people have had their embarrassing moments, perhaps even more than the rest of us. They do not give up ... and neither should we. Get over it and get on with the rest of your life.

ERIC LIDDELL

In Edinburgh the Eric Liddell Centre is a place for old people and their carers to get together. Eric Liddell was a Scotsman, born in 1902 in China, where his parents were missionaries and teachers. He grew up in a boarding school in England, although his family home was in Edinburgh, and became a committed Christian himself. He served as a missionary in China from 1952 to 1943 and, in 1932, qualified as a minister.

China at this time was a very dangerous place, as a result of civil war and attacks from Japan. When the fighting with Japan became part of the Second World War after 1941, things became even more dangerous. Liddell was not put off. He had a bicycle and he cycled about the countryside preaching in small towns and villages. Few of the Chinese who listened to him can have known of his earlier career as an athlete.

As a young man, Liddell was Scotland's finest athlete. In 1923 he won the 100 and 220 yard sprints at the British championships. His 100 yards time stood as a record for 35 years. In the 1924 Paris Olympics he was a definite favourite for the 100 metres.

Then came a shock. On arriving in Paris it was discovered that the 100 metres heats were to take place on the Sunday. As a Christian, Liddell did not think it right to run on a Sunday so he withdrew from the race.

Instead, Liddell was entered for the 400 metres. This was not his speciality and no one expected any real success. On the day of the final, however he completed the one lap race in a world record time and beat the second placed runner by five metres. It was an astounding performance.

Eric Liddell is probably Scotland's greatest ever athlete, but it was his work in China that he considered to be really important. In 1943 he was imprisoned by the Japanese and in his internment camp he worked hard on behalf of his fellow prisoners. His own health, however, was now in rapid decline. A brain tumour caused him terrible pain and eventually killed him in 1945, seven months before the war ended. He was only 43 years old.

The lesson: Few people nowadays would withdraw from a sporting event because it was being held on a Sunday. But Eric Liddell lived a heroic life according to his faith and his values. Do we all know what our values are? Do we always live up to them? If we don't, and that's probably most of us, we should find inspiration in the life of Eric Liddell.

TIME
MANAGEMENT

Time management is about making the most of a very precious resource. In this section you will learn how to:

■ Identify how much time is available to you.

■ Plan your studying so that you avoid last minute panics.

■ Use time management crutches that will help you meet your targets.

■ Get it right on the day of the exam so that you give of your best.

HOW MUCH TIME DO I HAVE?

For as long as there have been things to do, people have been obsessed with time. It can drag painfully and it can rush past at blinding speed. When we are bored, there is just too much of it; when we are busy, there never seems to be enough. Generally human beings have shown themselves very good at wasting time, not nearly so successful at using it effectively.

Back in Roman times, the poet Horace urged people to 'seize the day'. In the nineteenth century, the American writer Henry Thoreau wrote: 'It's not enough to be busy. The question is: What are you busy about?' Nowadays, every bookshop has a shelf of books offering advice on time management … and they sell well!

So, if you feel you could use your time better, you are in good company.

We would all benefit if we could practise good time management. Just as being short of money can be very stressful, so running out of time can cause great anxiety as well. This is particularly true for exam candidates.

Studying for exams brings you hard up against the realities of time. Time can move so slowly when you are stuck with something that does not interest you. But time seems to speed up mercilessly when the exams get close and you have much still to do.

Consider the situation of a student who has 200 pages of notes to learn up in 20 days. They could:

1 get started immediately and learn ten pages a day

2 or delay for ten days and then have 20 pages a day to learn

3 or wait until there are only five days to go until the exam. This will mean mastering 40 pages a day.

Do you recognise this scenario? How much better is it to choose option 1? How often do we all end up with option 3 because of our bad time management?

If only we could go for option 1 and stick to it for the 20 days, we would absorb the information more effectively, understand better what we are reading and we would avoid the stress of leaving everything to the last minute. We would be able to sit the exam with a clear conscience knowing that we had prepared well.

So, how does the student…how do *you*…make sure that it is definitely going to be option 1?

Commitment

First of all, and most importantly, you need commitment. You really must want to manage your time.

With commitment, you will:

- give the techniques described below a chance to work for you
- definitely achieve more, even if it is not as much as you originally hoped for
- get a 'feel good' factor because you will know that you are more in control of your life.

Without commitment, you are unlikely to get much out of time management because the various techniques need to be practised until you become comfortable with them – that does take time in itself, and you have to make that time.

It's really a matter, therefore, of whether you want to live in a frantic state forever or whether you would like, at some point, to be properly in control of things. If it's the latter, and it surely is, then it might as well be now.

Identifying available time

So, with the commitment made, you must now set time aside to get *organised*. This means identifying how much time is available for you to manage.

This is not as simple as it seems. Many of the 24 hours in the day are not there for you to use as you please. In practice, you have little or no choice how you use many hours in the day. That does not mean that they are wasted hours, but your control over them is very limited.

The following example is based on a typical school day. It uses hours as dividing measures but it could be school periods.

00.00–1.00	Sleep
1.00–2.00	Sleep
2.00–3.00	Sleep
3.00–4.00	Sleep
4.00–5.00	Sleep
5.00–6.00	Sleep
6.00–7.00	Sleep
7.00–8.00	Shower/Breakfast/Dress
8.00–9.00	Travel
9.00–10.00	In class
10.00–11.00	In class
11.00–12.00	In class
12.00–13.00	In class
13.00–14.00	Lunch break
14.00–15.00	In class
15.00–16.00	In class
16.00–17.00	Travel
17.00–18.00	Evening meal
18.00–19.00	
19.00–20.00	Training
20.00–21.00	Training
21.00–22.00	
22.00–23.00	
23.00–24.00	Sleep

This section may be quite different from your friends depending on your family commitments, work and hobbies.

Marked in pink is what we call *committed* time. It is time we are committed to using in a particular way and which we cannot use for other purposes. We could try to do without sleep, but we would quickly suffer if we did. We need to eat and we need to wash. Travel takes time. If we do not want to be boring, we need interests and, if we have joined a club, then we will be expected to turn up for training/rehearsal sessions. Perhaps, when we are really pressed, we could skip a session but we know we should not.

Marked in yellow are the slots which we call *uncommitted* time. These are the times when there is more flexibility. The uncommitted slots are:

13.00–14.00 We could grab a sandwich and then go to the library to finish off some work. The truth is that we are unlikely to get in a full hour of work at this time.

21.00–23.00 This is marked as uncommitted time but it is just after training/rehearsals. We are likely to be tired, probably needing to sit down, relax and watch some television before bed.

All in all, the above example does not look a good day for private study and we will have to be sure that every day is not like this.

You need therefore to take an overview of the whole week (see *Using a planner* below) and look at how much uncommitted time you have across the seven days. It might look something like this:

	Mon	Tues	Wed	Thurs	Fri	Sat	Sun
00.00–1.00							
1.00–2.00							
2.00–3.00							
3.00–4.00							
4.00–5.00							
5.00–6.00							
6.00–7.00							
7.00–8.00							
8.00–9.00							
9.00–10.00							
10.00–11.00						Work	
11.00–12.00						Work	
12.00–13.00						Work	
13.00–14.00						Work	Training/ rehearsal
14.00–15.00						Work	Training/ rehearsal
15.00–16.00						Work	Training/ rehearsal
16.00–17.00						Work	
17.00–18.00						Work	
18.00–19.00							
19.00–20.00				Training/ rehearsal			
20.00–21.00				Training/ rehearsal			
21.00–22.00							
22.00–23.00							
23.00–24.00							

The yellow time slots are what matter. These are the *uncommitted* time periods. You will use them for:

- watching television
- going out
- going to a club or organisation
- lazing about
- etc., etc.
- *and for studying.*

You must identify a sensible number of hours for studying. You cannot study all the time, and it is important to have time off. But if you are serious about exam success, then the hours of studying have to be put in.

So, create your overview of a typical week by:

- drawing a blank weekly timetable like the one above
- inserting your committed time slots, the times you cannot change
- putting into the uncommitted slots all your other activities and interests
- identifying at least ten of these uncommitted hours which you will devote to studying

Then stick to your personalised timetable!

TIME MANAGEMENT CRUTCHES

If you break your leg, it is very difficult to get about and you will therefore need to use crutches. If you are trying to manage time, it is very difficult and you will therefore find it helpful to have some 'crutches', time management assistants or aids. If you have tremendous willpower, you might be able to do without these, but why should you? These are techniques which have been developed over the years, in some cases over centuries, and they have proved useful to very many people. So why should you not benefit from them as well? Give serious consideration to each in turn, perhaps try them out for a while, and then stick with the ones that work best for you.

Keeping a journal

Keeping a journal or diary lets you keep a check on your time management. In a few words, perhaps last thing at night, you can review how well you managed your time during the day. Write down the things you achieved. You may well have done more than you realised. You can also pen a few words to yourself about tomorrow, encouraging yourself to manage your time even better the following day. You will become your own trainer and coach.

By the way, you will have great fun in five years time reading about yourself and how you were determined to make the most of your time and achieve exam success. You never know, you might even be impressed by yourself and, in five, ten, 20 years, that might be just the personal boost you are needing, as you tackle the particular challenge you are facing at that time.

Using a forward planner

Perhaps a journal does not appeal to you, but you must at least keep a homework diary. You must know when homework is due, when your deadlines are and when the exams will take place. You must have an overview of what you are doing.

This section is deliberately called 'using a forward planner' rather than 'using a homework diary' because many schools now issue their pupils with more ambitious planners, or arrange for pupils to buy them at a nominal charge. Such planners allow you to note homework, to create 'To Do' lists (see below) and to mark key exam dates. Many are customised to the particular school and also therefore contain much other useful information about forthcoming events, school rules, canteen menus and the like.

There are very sophisticated planners available commercially, but these can be expensive and you can easily make up your own planner with a cheap ring binder and a few inserts (daily diary, 'To Do' list sheets, year overview, reading lists, address book, etc.). It will not look as good as something that costs £50 but it can be just as effective.

So long as you do use it! Planners need to be worked at. You must set time aside, when you first decide to use one, to get your priorities identified, key dates inserted and blocks of revision time clearly marked.

You also have to check it regularly not only to ensure you are on track but also because priorities can change and new dates may have to be added or old ones altered. Discipline is required to work a planner but, by the same token, a planner helps you to become a more disciplined individual and thus a more effective and ultimately successful student.

Using a 'To Do' list

'To Do' lists are incredibly useful and can also be very depressing. There are few things more satisfying than crossing off a task, marking it as 'done' or 'completed', and knowing that you have actually achieved something. But it can be very demotivating, at the end of a day, to look at a list which has nothing scored out or which looks as long as it did first thing in the morning. You should definitely use 'To Do' lists but you should use them sensibly and in a positive way so that they genuinely assist you to manage your time.

At one level, such lists are very simple. Look at this example:

1 record favourite TV programme

2 'chat' on internet to friends

3 do maths homework

4 go for a swim/workout

5 read 20 pages of English novel

6 watch TV

7 text/phone friend

8 get kit ready for training/rehearsal

9 do my ironing

10 walk the dog.

On the face of it, this is quite straightforward. It could be written on a scrap of paper (and a 'To Do' list should always be written down, as a reminder to yourself) and each item crossed off as it is overtaken. Perhaps, though, it could be made more efficient...and more motivating. Consider this version:

Category	*Task*
School	do maths homework read 20 pages of English novel
Fitness	go for a swim/workout
Social/Entertainment	speak to friends – phone/internet watch TV record favourite programme
Other	text/phone friend do ironing

Here the various tasks have been organised into categories. This gives you a better overview of your day and highlights whether you are perhaps doing too much on the social front and not enough on school work!

We could go further, however. We could categorise the tasks according to how essential they are. This is called *prioritisation* and more will be said about it shortly. For the moment, look at how the list could be further adapted:

Category	Task	Priority	Status
School	do maths homework	2	✓
	read 20 pages of *Lord of the Flies*	1	
Fitness	go for a swim/workout	2	
Social/ Entertainment	phone friends	1	
	watch TV	3	
	record favourite programme	1	✓
Other	get kit ready	2	✓
	do ironing	2	
	text/phone friend	3	✓
	walk dog	1	

Three orders of priority have been created:

- 1 = must do
- 2 = should do
- 3 = could be left.

Prioritising a 'To Do' list in this way encourages us to spend our time mainly on the things that are essential and less time of the things that do not matter so much.

In this example there is also a column in which you can put a tick to show that a task has been completed. It is not strictly necessary because a simple crossing-out of the task would do. Our example, however, does clearly show how the list maker is getting it wrong. Yes, he has completed a few tasks but not according to the prioritisation he originally set for himself. He should have focused on completing the priority 1 tasks. By failing to do so, he has probably stored up trouble for himself the following day and, looking at his list at the end of the day, he will be a bit disappointed in himself.

Here are some other tips on using 'To Do' lists:

- Keep the lists short.

- Give yourself a reasonable chance to overtake the tasks and be sensible about the number of 'must do' tasks, that is the number of '1s'.

- Use the forward planning techniques discussed earlier, to ensure you do not have too many 1s on any given day.

- Think about how long a task will take. Some tasks will involve you in possibly two hours work, others can be knocked off in two minutes.

- Some things have to be done at a certain time, or within certain time slots. You can only go for a swim when the pool is open, but you can get your kit ready anytime.

- Draw up your list last thing at night for the following morning. Leave a little space for new tasks that emerge in the course of the next day, but be very strict about adding more than one or two of these.

- With your list on the desk in front of you, or in your pocket as you move about, work your way steadily through what you want to do.

- Consider keeping your daily lists in your planner or in a 'To Do' notebook, rather than just on bits of paper which your later discard. Keeping your old lists and looking back on all the things you've achieved will further increase your satisfaction level and motivate you to work even more efficiently in the future.

- Consider also using a diary on your computer, if you have one. Electronic diaries are very powerful, are easy to customise to suit your purposes and usually incorporate a 'To Do' list facility. You might be able to synchronise your phone with your electronic diary so you can be reminded of your 'To Do' list when you're out.

Prioritising

There were several references to prioritisation in the previous section and it does need to be discussed in a little more detail.

The American self-help writer and lecturer, Stephen Covey, has developed a particularly useful approach to the subject. Covey thinks in terms of four quadrants as shown in the diagram below:

Not important Not urgent	Important Urgent
Not important Urgent	Important Not Urgent

Some things that we spend our time on are not very important in themselves and there is no urgency about doing them. If we keep putting them off, however, they do become urgent. Then we have to set time aside to deal with them and that can be very annoying because we know that we are devoting precious minutes or hours, possibly at an inconvenient time, to something that is essentially trivial.

Other things are definitely important, like handing in an exam project by the deadline. Good time management will enable that crucial task to be performed without alarm bells ringing. But bad time management will mean that the very important task is left to the last minute. Then there is real urgency and serious stress will kick in.

Look again at the coloured quadrants above. Covey's argument – and instinctively one feels he is right – is that most of us spend far too much of our time operating in the green quadrant and, as a result, often find ourselves being propelled into the blue quadrant and, much more seriously, into the red quadrant.

What we should be doing, of course, is spending most of our time in the yellow quadrant, getting on with the things that matter, but in a well-organised, non-urgent, focussed but unstressed, manner.

Our spare time should be spent in the green quadrant, relaxing and enjoying ourselves and ticking off little jobs in order to stay on top of them, ensuring they do not become matters of urgency.

Working with a time management partner

Sometimes it can be very hard sitting on your own trying to study, with the sun shining outside, or with the knowledge that you are missing a favourite TV programme, or because your friends are off to the cinema. Yes, it's hard and it seems very unfair. It *is* hard but it is not as unfair as you think. Do well in your exams and you will know that the sacrifices were worthwhile. Other people have to give up things as well, perhaps at the time when *you* are the one able to relax. These truths, however, offer little consolation at the time, when your resentment at your condition can distract you from effective studying.

One very powerful solution is to get a time management or study partner. Better still, get a study group together. Great benefits come to whole year groups when collectively they decide to do their best and to support each other. The contrast is with the pupil who wants to do well but is depressed by the apathy and sometimes rejection that surrounds him or her. But when a number of individuals all want to do their best, and also want everyone else in the group to do well, then a tremendous team spirit can develop and a mutual support system can take off.

This can work in several ways. For example, an individual who has been ill, or has lost their notes, or has become confused by a particularly difficult part of the course, can get help from a friend or friends in the group. The one who is struggling benefits but so also do the helpers because, in explaining the topic, they help reinforce it in their own minds.

And for the student swotting away in their bedroom, there is a little less loneliness if there is the sure and certain knowledge that their study friends are, at the very same time, studying away on *their* own. In this scenario, the group could even have agreed to get together for ten minutes on MSN at, say, 9.30pm.

Then there is the study group which goes to the library in the evening together. It is best that the students do not sit together but spread out using all the desks available. But they are all in the same room, all engaged in the same activity. Two hours hard graft and then the group can head home together, reflecting on what they have been studying, more likely just gossiping, perhaps going on to the Sports Centre together for a swim (a very good idea), drawing support from each other and knowing that they are all in it together.

Do not underestimate the power of this crutch – working with others.

Treating and bribing yourself

Everyone needs a treat, and there is no need to apologise for this crutch. We are human after all, not machines. We cannot just work and work and work. The whole thrust of time management is to work *effectively*, to produce quality work not simply to put in long hours.

But there are times when we all need to be motivated and to reinforce our commitment. Even the toughest can find both the flesh and the spirit weakening. So, give yourself a treat. If you work well through the week, if you do stick to your forward plan, if you do meet that deadline and you have crossed off the tasks on your 'To Do' list, then promise yourself a break and a treat. Take them and enjoy them. Well done!

By the way, if you've cheated and not really earned the treat your conscience won't allow you to enjoy it properly. But, if you *know* you've done the business, then you really will enjoy yourself because you will, quite rightly, be pleased with yourself. Your batteries will be recharged and you will be ready for the next bout of studying.

GETTING IT RIGHT...

You can manage your time over the course of a whole year, over a school term, over a week or even over a single day. If you wrote planners for all these periods, you would incorporate very different levels of detail, but the basic principles are the same. The most important thing is for you to be in control of your time as much as possible.

...for the term

The sooner you get started with time management, the better. You should certainly begin each new term at school by:

- checking your planner is up to date
- identifying when pressure points are likely to arise
- marking in particular days or weekends when special events are taking place which might disrupt your normal study schedule
- establishing clear personal goals that you want to achieve by the end of the term.

...for the week

At the beginning of every week, perhaps on the Sunday evening before you go back to school, establish what you have to do in the next seven days.

- use your planner to get an overview of the whole week
- be clear what homework is due on which days and when you are going to do it
- check that you will be able to keep to your study schedule ... or have special circumstances arisen?

- prepare your first 'To Do' list of the week (and remember to check and revise it at the end of each day)
- ask yourself: what am I going to do this week, which will help me achieve my personal goals for the term?

...on the day of the exam

You have worked hard for your exams and now you want to be at your very best on the big day. You will have sat Prelims, had plenty of practice with past papers, and now you are determined not to let yourself down in the real thing. Here are some useful hints to help you produce a peak performance on the big day.

Have a clear conscience
In other words, know that you have studied hard and, if you do not get the mark you would like, then it will not be because of lack of effort.

Avoid unnecessary upsets in the run-up to the exams
Try not to break up with your girl or boyfriend in the weeks before the exam. Do not fall out with your parents if you can possibly avoid it. Avoid quarrels with other pupils. All these things are very upsetting and will distract you from concentrating on your studies.

Get a good night's sleep
Some students have done well by studying all night and then sitting their exam the following morning. Such individuals are very rare. If you have worked hard in the time leading up to the exam, then you should stop studying at a sensible time the evening before. Have a relaxing bath. Perhaps watch a little television. Then get to bed and have a full eight hours sleep. Exams are demanding and you will need lots of energy for the intellectual and physical effort required. That means your body needs to be rested beforehand.

Have a decent, nourishing breakfast
This can be difficult. If you are nervous, it can put you off your food. But your body and brain require nourishment just as much as sleep. Try to eat something. Even a little is better than nothing. Perhaps you could take a cereal bar with you to school because you might feel like it later. Always remember to drink water.

Have all the necessary equipment to hand
Pens, pencils, rulers, calculators – have them all laid out the night before and make sure you take them with you in the morning.

Get to the exam on time

This does not mean too early. Talking too much to others before the exam can be off-putting. You cannot believe what people say about the amount of studying they have done. But, whether you believe them or not, you could easily find their conversation unsettling. Be at the exam room five to ten minutes before you are required to be there. That way you will not be rushed, you will have time to do a final check that you've got everything you need and to confirm your seat number, but not so much time that you will begin worrying. If you do find the tension becoming unbearable, go to a quiet place and breathe deeply and slowly to relax yourself. Or go and talk to a friendly teacher (they do exist!). All teachers had to go through the exam process themselves and will know how you are feeling.

Listen to the Invigilator

You will given instructions by the exam's Chief Invigilator. These instructions are important, so give this man or woman your full attention. He or she wants you to do well and does not wish you to be penalised in any way.

Remember the advice on tackling the exam

When the exam finally begins, and you are allowed to open the question paper, do not forget the techniques you have been practising. Read the questions carefully, underlining or highlighting key words and statistics; plan your answers before you start writing, perhaps by drawing a quick mind-map; check your watch regularly and make sure you do not run out of time; if you forget important information, do not panic but instead calmly use your memory techniques to bring things back into your mind; keep thinking throughout because if you switch to autopilot you may miss subtleties in the question and your answers will lack sparkle.

After the exam

Put it behind you, because there is now nothing you can do about it. Do not discuss it with your friends afterwards, because it will just depress you if their answers are different from yours. You will be tired and you are unlikely to remember clearly what you have written, anyway. What's done is done. Move on to the next exam. Or, if you are finished altogether, celebrate. If you have followed all the advice in this book, you will deserve to.

CHAPTER SUMMARY

What's In It For Me!

Time is precious. If you practise time management, you will:

- get more out of your day because you will be making more efficient use of your time
- reduce your stress levels because you feel in control of your life
- feel good about yourself because of what you will have achieved
- enjoy your leisure time far more, because you will have earned it.

But you need to work at time management; it requires a lot of self discipline. To help you there are a many 'crutches' available. Use them.

Further reading

You can learn more about how to look after yourself from the following books:

- J Oliver *Jamie's Dinners* 2004, Michael Joseph
  Jamie Oliver received a lot of publicity in 2005 when he criticised the quality of many school meals and the diet of teenagers. So, you might find this book useful.

- C L Wiatt and B Schroeder *The Diet for Teenagers Only* 2005, Regan Books

- K Gaede *Fitness Training for Girls: A Teen Girl's Guide to Resistance Training, Cardiovascular Conditioning and Nutrition* 2001, Tracks Publishing
  Bookshops have a huge number of books on physical fitness. This one is aimed specially for girls.

If you want to explore reading and note-taking ideas in more depth, the following are recommended…

- T Konstant *Speed Reading* 2003, Teach Yourself paperback
  Tina Konstant has worked in schools discussing her books on effective reading with pupils who have to do a lot of reading for their exams.

- T Buzan *Use Your Head* 2003, BBC Books
  Tony Buzan is the great expert on mind-mapping and he has written many books on the subject. There is a very easy and colourful introduction to the subject for young people but it is probably too juvenile for you, so go for the adult version listed above.

For online information about mind-mapping and other learning techniques, have a look at the Leckie & Leckie Learning Lab:

- http://www.leckieandleckie.co.uk/learning_lab/learning_lab.asp

- http://www.3mrt.com

If you are interested in managing your time and in your personal development generally, you could try….

- S Covey *The 7 Habits of Highly Effective Teenagers* 2004, Simon & Schuster
  Sean Covey's father wrote the famous and much quoted personal development book Seven Habits of Highly Effective People. Sean has entertainingly adapted his father's book for teenagers.

- A Robbins *Notes From a Friend* 2004, Pocket Books
  Anthony Robbins is as famous as Stephen Covey. He has written two, very long personal development books. This, however, is a short introduction to his ideas.

- J Gray *Men Are from Mars, Women Are from Venus: How to Get What You Want in Your Relationship* 2002, HarperCollins
  A classic and unique self-help book tackling the perennial problems faced by couples everywhere.

If you are having difficulty in getting past papers, you can order them directly from the publishers, Leckie & Leckie:

- http://www.leckieandleckie.co.uk/